The Van Dv

A Strenuous Quest for a Home

Albert Bigelow Paine

Alpha Editions

This edition published in 2024

ISBN : 9789362929105

Design and Setting By
Alpha Editions
www.alphaedis.com
Email - info@alphaedis.com

As per information held with us this book is in Public Domain.
This book is a reproduction of an important historical work. Alpha Editions uses the best technology to reproduce historical work in the same manner it was first published to preserve its original nature. Any marks or number seen are left intentionally to preserve its true form.

Contents

I. ....- 1 -
II. ....- 5 -
III. ....- 10 -
IV. ....- 15 -
V. ....- 21 -
VI. ....- 25 -
VII. ....- 29 -
VIII. ....- 30 -
IX. ....- 36 -
X. ....- 39 -
XI. ....- 45 -
XII. ....- 51 -
XIII. ....- 58 -
XIV. ....- 61 -

I.

The First Home in the Metropolis.

We had never lived in New York. This fact will develop anyway, as I proceed, but somehow it seems fairer to everybody to state it in the first sentence and have it over with.

Still, we had heard of flats in a vague way, and as we drew near the Metropolis the Little Woman bought papers of the train boy and began to read advertisements under the head of "Flats and Apartments to Let."

I remember that we wondered then what was the difference. Now, having tried both, we are wiser. The difference ranges from three hundred dollars a year up. There are also minor details, such as palms in the vestibule, exposed plumbing, and uniformed hall service—perhaps an elevator, but these things are immaterial. The price is the difference.

We bought papers, as I have said. It was the beginning of our downfall, and the first step was easy—even alluring. We compared prices and descriptions and put down addresses. The descriptions were all that could be desired and the prices absurdly modest. We had heard that living in the city was expensive; now we put down the street and number of "four large light rooms and improvements, $18.00," and were properly indignant at those who had libeled the landlords of Gotham.

Next morning we stumbled up four dim flights of stairs, groped through a black passage-way and sidled out into a succession of gloomy closets, wondering what they were for. Our conductor stopped and turned.

"This is it," he announced. "All nice light rooms, and improvements."

It was our first meeting with a flat. Also, with a janitor. The Little Woman was first to speak.

"Ah, yes, would you mind telling us—we're from the West, you know—just which are the—the improvements, and which the rooms?"

This was lost on the janitor. He merely thought us stupid and regarded us with pitying disgust as he indicated a rusty little range, and disheartening water arrangements in one corner. There may have been stationary tubs, too, bells, and a dumb waiter, but without the knowledge of these things which we acquired later they escaped notice. What we *could* see was that there was no provision for heat that we could discover, and no sunshine.

We referred to these things, also to the fact that the only entrance to our parlor would be through the kitchen, while the only entrance to our kitchen would be almost certainly over either a coal-box, an ironing board, or the rusty little stove, any method of which would require a certain skill, as well as care in the matter of one's clothes.

But these objections seemed unreasonable, no doubt, for the janitor, who was of Yorkshire extraction, became taciturn and remarked briefly that the halls were warmed and that nobody before had ever required more heat than they got from these and the range, while as for the sun, he couldn't change that if he wanted to, leaving us to infer that if he only wanted to he could remodel almost everything else about the premises in short order.

We went away in the belief that he was a base pretender, "clad in a little brief authority." We had not awakened as yet to the fulness of janitorial tyranny and power.

We went farther uptown. We reasoned that rentals would be more reasonable and apartments less contracted up there.

Ah, me! As I close my eyes now and recall, as in a kaleidoscope, the perfect wilderness of flats we have passed through since then, it seems strange that some dim foreboding of it all did not steal in to rob our hearts of the careless joys of anticipation.

But I digress. We took the elevated and looked out the windows as we sped along. The whirling streets, with their endless procession of front steps, bewildered us.

By and by we were in a vast district, where all the houses were five-storied, flat-roofed, and seemed built mainly to hold windows. This was Flatland— the very heart of it—that boundless territory to the northward of Central Park, where nightly the millions sleep.

Here and there were large signs on side walls and on boards along the roof, with which we were now on a level as the train whirled us along. These quoted the number of rooms, and prices, and some of them were almost irresistible. "6 All Light Rooms, $22.00," caught us at length, and we got off to investigate.

They were better than those downtown. There was a possibility of heat and you did not get to the parlor by climbing over the kitchen furniture. Still, the apartment as a whole lacked much that we had set our hearts on, while it contained some things that we were willing to do without.

It contained, also, certain novelties. Among these were the stationary washtubs in the kitchen; the dumb-waiter, and a speaking-tube connection with the basement.

The janitor at this place was a somber Teutonic female, soiled as to dress, and of the common Dutch-slipper variety.

We were really attracted by the next apartment, where we discovered for the first time the small button in the wall that, when pressed, opens the street door below. This was quite jolly, and we played with it some minutes, while the colored janitor grinned at our artlessness, and said good things about the place. Our hearts went out to this person, and we would gladly have cast our lot with him.

Then he told us the price, and we passed on.

I have a confused recollection of the other flats and apartments we examined on that first day of our career, or "progress," as the recent Mr. Hogarth would put it. Our minds had not then become trained to that perfection of mentality which enables the skilled flat-hunter to carry for days visual ground-plans, elevations, and improvements, of any number of "desirable apartments," and be ready to transcribe the same in black and white at a moment's notice.

I recall one tunnel and one roof garden. Also one first floor with bake-shop attachment. The latter suggested a business enterprise for the Little Woman, while the Precious Ones, who were with us at this stage, seemed delighted at my proposition of "keeping store."

Many places we did not examine. Of these the janitors merely popped out their heads—frowsy heads, most of them—and gave the number of rooms and the price in a breath of defiance and mixed ale. At length I was the only one able to continue the search.

I left the others at a friendly drug store, and wandered off alone. Being quite untrammeled now I went as if by instinct two blocks west and turned. A park was there—a park set up on edge, as it were, with steps leading to a battlement at the top. This was attractive, and I followed along opposite, looking at the houses. Presently I came to a new one. They were just finishing it, and sweeping the shavings from the ground-floor flat—a gaudy little place—the only one in the house untaken.

It was not very light, and it was not very large, while the price was more than we had expected to pay. But it was clean and new, and the landlord, who was himself on the premises, offered a month's rent free to the first tenant.

I ran all the way back to the Little Woman, and urged her to limp as hastily as possible, fearing it might be gone before she could get there. When I realized that the landlord had held it for me in the face of several applicants (this was his own statement), I was ready to fall on his neck, and paid a deposit hastily to secure the premises.

Then we wandered about looking at things, trying the dumb waiter, the speaking tube, and the push-button, leading to what the Precious Ones promptly named the "locker-locker" door, owing to a clicking sound in the lock when the door sprang open.

We were in a generous frame of mind, and walked from room to room praising the excellence of everything, including a little gingerbread mantel in the dining-room, in which the fireplace had been set crooked,—from being done in the dark, perhaps,—the concrete backyard, with its clothesline pole, the decorated ceilings, the precipitous park opposite that was presently to shut off each day at two P.M. our western, and only, sunlight; even the air-shaft that came down to us like a well from above, and the tiny kitchen, which in the gathering evening was too dark to reveal all its attractions.

As for the Precious Ones, they fairly raced through our new possession, shrieking their delight.

We had a home in the great city at last.

II.

Metropolitan Beginnings.

We set out gaily and early, next morning, to buy our things.

We had brought nothing with us that could not be packed into our trunks, except my fishing rod, some inherited bedding and pictures which the Little Woman declined to part with, and two jaded and overworked dolls belonging to the Precious Ones. Manifestly this was not enough to begin housekeeping on, even in a flat of contracted floor-space and limitless improvements.

In fact the dolls only had arrived. They had come as passengers. The other things were still trundling along somewhere between Oshkosh and Hoboken, by slow freight.

We had some idea of where we wanted to go when we set forth, but a storehouse with varied and almost irresistible windows enticed us and we went no farther. It was a mighty department store and we were informed that we need not pass its doors again until we had selected everything we needed from a can-opener to a grand piano. We didn't, and the can-opener became ours.

Also other articles. We enjoyed buying things, and even to this day I recall with pleasure our first great revel in a department store.

For the most part we united our judgments and acted jointly. But at times we were enticed apart by fascinating novelties and selected recklessly, without consultation.

As for the Precious Ones, they galloped about, demanding that we should buy everything in sight, with a total disregard of our requirements or resources.

It was wonderful though how cheap everything seemed, and how much we seemed to need, even for a beginning. It was also wonderful how those insidious figures told in the final settlement.

Let it be understood, I cherish no resentment toward the salesmen. Reflecting now on the matter, I am, on the whole, grateful. They found out where we were from, and where we were going to live, and they sold us accordingly.

I think we interested them, and that they rather liked us. If not, I am sure they would have sold us worse things and more of them. They could have done so, easily. Hence my gratitude to the salesmen; but the man at the transfer desk remains unforgiven.

I am satisfied, now, that he was an unscrupulous person, a perjured, case-hardened creature whom it is every man's duty to destroy. But at the time he seemed the very embodiment of good intentions.

He assured us heartily, as he gave us our change, that we should have immediate delivery. We had explained at some length that this was important, and why. He waved us off with the assurance that we need give ourselves no uneasiness in the matter—that, in all probability, the matting we had purchased as a floor basis would be there before we were.

He knew that this would start us post-haste for our apartment, which it did. We even ran, waving and shouting, after a particular car when another just like it was less than a half block behind.

We breathed more easily when we arrived at our new address and found that we were in good season. When five minutes more had passed, however, and still no signs of our matting, a vague uneasiness began to manifest itself.

It was early and there was plenty of time, of course; but there was something about the countless delivery wagons that passed and re-passed without stopping which impressed us with the littleness of our importance in this great whirl of traffic, and the ease with which a transfer clerk's promise, easily and cheerfully made, might be as easily and as cheerfully forgotten.

I said presently that I would go around the corner and order coal for the range, ice for the refrigerator, and groceries for us all. I added that the things from down town would surely be there on my return, and that any way I wanted to learn where the nearest markets were. Had I known it, I need not have taken this trouble. Our names in the mail-box just outside the door would have summoned the numerous emissaries of trade, as if by magic.

It did so, in fact, for the Little Woman put the name in while I was gone, and on my return I found her besieged by no less than three butchers and grocerymen, while two rival milkmen were explaining with diagrams the comparative richness of their respective cans and bottles. The articles I had but just purchased were even then being sent up on the dumb waiter, but our furnishings from below were still unheard from.

A horrible fear that I had given the wrong address began to grow upon us. The Little Woman was calm, but regarded me accusingly. She said she didn't see how it could have happened, when in every accent of her voice I could detect memories of other things I had done in this line—things which, at the time, had seemed equally impossible.

She said she hadn't been paying attention when I gave the number or she would have known. Of course, she said, the transfer clerk couldn't make a mistake putting it down—he was too accustomed to such things, and of course I must have given it to him correctly—only, it did seem strange——

We began debating feverishly as to the advisability of my setting out at once on a trip down town to see about it. We concluded to telephone.

I hastened around to the drug store not far away and "helloed" and repeated and fumed and swore in agony for half an hour, but I came back in high spirits. The address was correct and the delivery wagons were out. I expected to find them at the door when I got back, but found only the Little Woman, sitting on the doorstep, still waiting.

We told each other that after all it must necessarily take some little time to get up this far, but that the matting would certainly be along presently, now, and that it would take but a short time to lay it.

Then we would have a good start, and even if everything didn't come tonight it would be jolly to put the new mattresses down on the nice clean matting, and to get dinner the best way we could—like camping out. Then we walked back and forth in the semi-light of our empty little place and said how nice it was, and where we should set the furniture and hang the pictures: and stepped off the size of the rooms that all put together were not so big as had been our one big sitting-room in the West.

As for the Precious Ones, they were wildly happy. They had never had a real playhouse before, big enough to live in, and this was quite in accordance with their ideals. They were "visiting" and "keeping store" and "cooking," and quarreling, and having a perfectly beautiful time with their two disreputable dolls, utterly regardless of the shadow of foreboding and desolation that grew ever thicker as the hours passed, while the sun slipped down behind the steep stone-battlemented park opposite, and brought no matting, no furniture, no anything that would make our little nest habitable for the swiftly coming night.

But when it became too dark for them to see to play, they came clamorously out to where we stood on the doorstep, still waiting, and demanded in one breath that we tell them immediately when the things were coming, where they were to get supper, how we were to sleep, and if they couldn't have a light.

I was glad that I could give them something. I said that it was pretty early for a light, but that they should have it. I went in and opened a gas burner, and held a match to it. There was no result. I said there was air in the pipes. I lit another match, and held it till it burned my fingers. There was air in the pipes, I suppose, but there was no gas. I hurried down to inform the janitor.

She was a stern-featured Hibernian, with a superior bearing. I learned later that she had seen better days. In fact, I have yet to find the janitor that *hasn't* seen better days, or the tenant, either, for that matter, but this is another digression. She regarded me with indifference when I told her there was no gas. When I told her that we *wanted* gas, she inspected me as if this was something unusual and interesting in a tenant's requirements. Finally she said:—

"Well, and when did yez order it turned on?"

"Why," I said, "I haven't ordered it at all. I thought——"

"Yez thought you could get it of me, did yez?"

I admitted that this seemed reasonable, but in view of the fact of the water being turned on, I had really given the matter of gas no deliberate consideration.

I think she rather pitied my stupendous ignorance. At least she became more gentle than she had seemed at the start, or than she ever was afterwards.

She explained at some length that I must go first to the gas office, leave a deposit to secure them, in case of my sudden and absent-minded departure from the neighborhood, and ask that a man be sent around to put in a meter, and turn on the gas in our apartment. With good luck some result might be obtained by the following evening.

I stumbled miserably up the dark stairs, and dismally explained, while the Precious Ones became more clamorous for food and light, as the shades of night gathered. I said I would go and get some candles, so in case the things came—not necessarily the matting—we didn't really need the matting first, anyway—it would get scuffed and injured if it were put down first—it was the other things we needed—things to eat and go to bed with!—

When I came back there was a wild excitement around our entrance. A delivery wagon had driven up in great haste, and by the light of the street lamp I recognized on it the sign of our department store. A hunted-looking driver had leaped out and was hastily running over his book. Yes, it was our name—our things had come at last—better late than never! The driver was diving back into his wagon and presently hauled out something long and round and wrapped up.

"Here you are," he said triumphantly. "Sign for it, please."

"But," we gasped, "where's the rest of the things? There's ever so much more."

"Don't know, lady. This is all I've got. Sign please, it's getting late."

"But——"

He was gone. We carried in our solitary package and opened it by the feeble flickering of a paraffine dip.

It was a Japanese umbrella-holder!

The Precious Ones and their wretched dolls held a war dance around it and admired the funny men on the sides. To us it was an Oriental mockery.

Sadly we gathered up our bags, and each taking by the hand a hungry little creature who clasped a forlorn doll to a weary little bosom, we set forth to seek food and shelter in the thronging but pitiless city.

III.

Learning by Experience.

Day by day, and piece by piece, our purchases appeared. Now and then a delivery wagon would drive up in hot haste and deliver a stew-pan, or perhaps a mouse trap. At last, and on the third day, a mattress.

Of course, I had been down and protested, ere this. The cheerful liar at the transfer desk had been grieved, astonished, thunderstruck at my tale. He would investigate, and somebody would be discharged, at once. This thought soothed me. It was blood that I wanted. Just plain blood, and plenty of it. I know now that it was the transfer-man's blood, that I needed, but for the moment I was appeased and believed in him.

Our matting, promised within two hours from the moment of purchase, was the last thing to arrive. This on the fourth day—or was it the fifth? I was too mad by this time to remember dates. What I do recall is that we laid it ourselves. We had not, as yet, paid for the laying, and we said that rather than give that shameless firm another dollar we would lay that matting if it killed us.

Morally it did. I have never been quite the same man since that terrible experience. The Little Woman helped stretch, and held the lamp, while I pounded my thumb and swore. She said she had never realized until that night how well and satisfactorily I could swear. It seemed to comfort her and she abetted it.

I know now that the stripes on matting never match. We didn't know it then, and we tried to make them. We pulled and hauled, and I got down on my stomach, with one ear against the wall, and burned the other one on the lamp chimney which the Little Woman, in her anxiety to help, held too close. When I criticised her inclination to overdo matters, she observed that I would probably be able to pull the matting along more easily if I wouldn't lie down on the piece I was trying to pull. Then we both said some things that I suppose we shall regret to our dying day. It was a terrible night. When morning came, grim and ghastly, life seemed a failure, and I could feel that I had grown old.

But with breakfast and coffee and sunshine came renewed hope.

We were settled at last, and our little place looked clean and more like a playhouse than ever.

Our acquaintance with the janitor was not, as yet, definite. I had met her once or twice informally, it is true, but as yet we could not be said to have reached any basis of understanding. As to her appearance, she was brawny and Irish, with a forbidding countenance. She had a husband whom we never saw—he being employed outside—but whose personality, nevertheless, became a factor in our subsequent relations.

Somehow, we instinctively avoided the people below stairs, as cats do canines, though we had no traditions concerning janitors, and we are naturally the most friendly and democratic people in the world.

Matters went on very well for a time. We congratulated ourselves every morning on how nice and handy everything was, now that we were once settled, and laughed over our recent difficulties. The Precious Ones were in their glory. They had appropriated the little four-by-six closet back of the kitchen—it had been shown to us as a servant's room—and presently we heard them playing "dumb waiter," "janitor," "locker-locker door," "laying matting," and other new and entertaining games incidental to a new life and conditions. The weather remained warm for a time, and it was all novel and interesting. We added almost daily to our household effects, and agreed that we had been lucky in securing so pleasant and so snug a nest.

But one morning when we awoke it was cold. It was early October, but there was a keen frosty feeling in the air that sent us shivering to the kitchen range, wondering if steam would be coming along presently. It did not come, and after breakfast I went down to interview our janitor on the subject.

I could see that she was not surprised at my errand. The incident of the gas supply had prepared her for any further eccentricity on my part. She merely waited with mild interest to hear what I really could do when I tried. Then she remarked tersely:—

"Yez get steam on the fifteenth."

"Quite so," I assented, "but it's cold to-day. We may not want it on the fifteenth. We do want it now."

These facts did not seem to impress her.

"Yez get steam on the fifteenth," she repeated, with even more decision, and I could tell from her manner that the interview was closed.

I went back to where the Little Woman was getting breakfast (she had laughed at the idea of a servant in our dainty little nest) and during the morning she and the Precious Ones hugged the kitchen range. In the afternoon the sun looked in at our parlor windows and made the room cheerful for an hour. Then it went out behind the precipitous hillside park opposite, and with the chill shadow that crept up over our windows came a foreboding that was bad for the romance and humor of the situation. It had been like a spiritless Arctic day.

In the evening we crept to the kitchen range; and we hibernated there, more or less, while the cold spell lasted. It was warm by the fifteenth, but on that day, in the hours of early dawn, we were awakened by a Wagnerian overture in the steam radiators. It became an anvil chorus ere long and there was no more sleep. By breakfast time we had all the things open that we could get open to let in fresh air and we were shouting to each other above the din and smell of the new pipes. We made allowance, of course, for the fact that things *were* new, and we said we were glad there would be enough heat in cold weather, anyway, by which you will see how really innocent we were in those days.

It grew cold in earnest by November first. And then, all at once, the gold-painted radiators, as if they had shown what they could do and were satisfied, seemed to lose enthusiasm. Now and then in the night, when we didn't want it, they would remember and start a little movement Fromm the Gotterdammerung, but by morning they seemed discouraged again and during the day they were of fitful and unresponsive temperature.

At last I went once more to the janitor, though with some hesitation, I confess. I don't know why. I am not naturally timid, and usually demand and obtain the rights of ordinary citizenship. Besides, I was ignorant then of janitorial tyranny as the accepted code. It must have been instinct. I said:—

"What's the matter with our heat up-stairs?"

She answered:—

"An' it's what's the matter with yer heat, is it? Well, thin, an' what *is* the matter with yer heat up-stairs?"

She said this, and also looked at me, as if she thought our heat might be afflicted with the mumps or measles or have a hare lip, and as if I was to blame for it.

"The matter is that we haven't got any," I said, getting somewhat awakened.

She looked at me fully a minute this time.

"Yez haven't got any! Yez haven't got any heat! An' here comes the madam from the top floor yesterday, a bilin' over, an' sayin that they're sick with *too much* heat. What air yez, then, sallymandhers?"

"But yesterday isn't to-day," I urged, "and I'm not the woman on the top floor. We're just the people on the first floor and we're cold. We want heat, not comparisons."

I wonder now how I was ever bold enough to say these things. It was my ignorance, of course. I would not dream of speaking thus disrespectfully to a janitor to-day. I had a dim idea at the time that the landlord had something to do with his own premises, and that if heat were not forthcoming I could consult him and get action in the matter. I know better than that, now, and my enlightenment on this point was not long delayed.

It was about twelve o'clock that night, I think, that we were aroused by a heart-breaking, furniture-smashing disturbance. At first I thought murder was being done on our doorstep. Then I realized that it was below us. I sat up in bed, my hair prickling. The Little Woman, in the next room with the Precious Ones, called to me in a voice that was full of emotion. I answered, "Sh!"

Then we both sat still in the dark while our veins grew icy. Somebody below was begging and pleading for mercy, while somebody else was commanding quiet in a voice that meant bloodshed as an alternative. At intervals there was a fierce struggle, mingled with destruction and hair-lifting language.

Was the janitor murdering her husband? Or could it be that it was the other way, and that tardy justice had overtaken the janitor—that, at the hands of her husband or some outraged tenant, she was meeting a well-merited doom? Remembering her presence and muscular proportions I could not hope that this was possible.

The Little Woman whispered tremblingly that we ought to do something. I whispered back that I was quite willing she should, if she wanted to, but that for my own part I had quit interfering in Hibernian domestic difficulties some years since. In the morning I would complain to the landlord of our service. I would stand it no longer.

Meantime, it was not yet morning, and the racket below went on. The very quantity of it was reassuring. There was too much of it for real murder. The Precious Ones presently woke up and cried. None of us got to sleep again until well-nigh morning, even after the commotion below had degenerated into occasional moans, and final silence.

Before breakfast I summoned up all my remaining courage and went down there. The janitor herself came to the door. She was uninjured, so far as I could discover. I was pretty mad, and the fact that I was afraid of her made me madder.

"What do you mean?" I demanded, "by making such a horrible racket down here in the middle of the night?"

She regarded me with an amazed look, as if I had been dreaming.

"I want to know," I repeated, "what was all that noise down here last night?"

She smiled grimly.

"Oh, an' is *that* it? Yez want to know what was the *ni'se*, do yez? Well, thin, it was none o' yer business, *that's* what it was. Now go on wid yez, an' tend to yer *own* business, if yez have any. D'y' mind?"

With the information that I was going at once to the landlord, I turned and hurried up the stairs to avoid violence. She promptly followed me.

"So yez'll be after telling the landlord, will yez? Well, thin, yez can just tell the landlord, an' yez can just sind him to me. You'll sind Tim Reilly to me. Maybe yez don't know that Tim Reilly once carried bricks fer my old daddy, an' many's the time I've given him a bite an' a sup at our back door. Oh, yes, sind him to me. Sind Tim Reilly to me, an' I'll see, when me ol' man comes home late wid a bit of liquor in his head, if it's not for me to conthrol 'im after our own fashions, widout the inquisitin' of people who better be mindin' of their own n'ise. Kep' yez awake, eh? Well, thin, see that yez never keep anybody else awake, an' sind Tim Reilly to me!"

She was gone. We realized then that she had seen better days. So had we. Later, when I passed her on the front steps, she nodded in her usual expressionless, uncompromising manner.

I did not go to the landlord. It would be useless, we said. The helplessness of our position was becoming daily more evident.

And with the realization of this we began to discover other defects. We found that the house faced really almost north instead of west, and that the sun now went behind the precipice opposite nearly as soon as it touched the tops of our windows, while the dining-room and kitchen were wretchedly dark all day long.

Then, too, the crooked fireplace in the former was a disfigurement, the rooms were closets, or cells, the paper abominable, the wardrobe damp, the drawers swollen or exasperating muftis, the whole apartment the flimsiest sort of a cheap, showy, contract structure, such as no self-respecting people should occupy.

We said we would move. We recited our wrongs to each other in detail and began consulting Sunday papers immediately.

IV.

Our First Move.

It was the Little Woman who selected our next habitation. Education accumulates rapidly in the Metropolis, and I could see that she already possessed more definite views on "flats and apartments" than she had acquired on many another subject familiar to her from childhood.

Politics, for instance, do not exist for the Little Woman. Presidents come and go, torchlight processions bloom and fade and leave not so much as a windriffle on the sands of memory. The stock market, too, was at this time but a name to her. Both of us have acquired knowledge since in this direction, but that is another story. Shares might rise and fall in those early days, and men clutch at each other's throats as ruin dragged them down. The Little Woman saw but a page of figures in the evening paper and perhaps regarded them as a sort of necessary form—somewhat in the nature of the congressional reports which nobody ever reads. Yet all her life she had been amid these vital issues, and now, behold, after two short months she had acquired more information on New York apartment life than she would ever have on both the others put together. She knew now what we needed and she would find it. I was willing that this should be so. There were other demands on my time, and besides, I had not then contracted the flat-disease in its subsequent virulent form.

She said, and I agreed with her, that it was a mistake to be so far from the business center. That the time, car fare, and nerve tissue wasted between Park Place and Harlem were of more moment than a few dollars' difference in the monthly rent.

We regarded this conclusion somewhat in the light of a discovery, and wondered why people of experience had not made it before. Ah, me! we have made many discoveries since that time. Discoveries as old as they are always new. The first friendly ray of March sunlight; the first green leaf in the park; the first summer glow of June; the first dead leaf and keen blast of autumn; these, too, have wakened within us each year a new understanding of our needs and of the ideal habitation; these, too, have set us to discovering as often as they come around, as men shall still discover so long as seasons of snow and blossom pass, and the heart of youth seeks change. But here I am digressing again, when I should be getting on with my story.

As I have said, the Little Woman selected our next home. The Little Woman and the Precious Ones. They were gone each day for several hours and returned each evening wearied to the bone but charged heavily with information.

The Little Woman was no longer a novice. "Single and double flats," "open plumbing," "tiled vestibule," "uniformed hall service," and other stock terms, came trippingly from her tongue.

Of some of the places she had diagrams. Of others she volunteered to draw them from memory. I did not then realize that this was the first symptom of flat-collecting in its acute form, or that in examining her crude pencilings I was courting the infection. I could not foresee that the slight yet definite and curious variation in the myriad city apartments might become a fascination at last, and the desire for possession a mania more enslaving than even the acquirement of rare rugs or old china and bottles.

I examined the Little Woman's assortment with growing interest while the Precious Ones chorused their experiences, which consisted mainly in the things they had been allowed to eat and drink, and from the nature of these I suspected occasional surrender and bribery on the part of the Little Woman.

It was a place well down town that we chose. It was a second floor, open in the rear, and there was sunlight most of the day. The rooms were really better than the ones we had. They could not be worse, we decided—a fallacy, for I have never seen a flat so bad that there could not be a worse one—and the price was not much higher. Also, there was a straight fireplace in the dining-room, which the Precious Ones described as being "lovelly," and the janitress was a humble creature who had won the Little Woman's heart by unburdening herself of numerous sad experiences and bitter wrongs, besides a number of perfectly just opinions concerning janitors, individually and at large.

Altogether the place seemed quite in accordance with our present views. I paid a month's rent in advance the next morning, and during the day the Little Woman engaged a moving man.

THE PRECIOUS ONES WERE RACING ABOUT AMONG BOXES AND BARRELS IN UNALLOYED HAPPINESS.

She was packing when I came home and the Precious Ones were racing about among boxes and barrels in unalloyed happiness. It did not seem possible that we had bought so much or that I could have put so many tacks in the matting.

The moving men would be there with their van by daylight next morning, she said. (It seems that the man at the office had told her that we would have to get up early to get ahead of him, and she had construed this statement literally.) So we toiled far into the night and then crept wearily to bed in our dismantled nest, to toss wakefully through the few remaining hours of darkness, fearful that the summons of the forehanded and expeditious moving man would find us in slumber and unprepared.

We were deeply grateful to him that he had not arrived before we had finished our early and scrappy breakfast. Then presently, when we were ready for him and he did not appear, we were still appreciative, for we said to each other that he was giving us a little extra time so that we would not feel upset and hurried. Still, it would be just as well if he would come, now, so that we might get moved and settled before night.

It had been a bright, pleasant morning, but as the forenoon advanced the sky darkened and it grew bitterly cold. Gloom settled down without and the meager steam supply was scarcely noticeable in our bare apartment. The Precious Ones ran every minute to the door to watch for the moving van and came back to us with blue noses and icy hands. We began to wonder if something had gone wrong. Perhaps a misunderstanding of the address—illness or sudden death on the part of the man who had made the engagement—perhaps—

I went around at last to make inquiries. A heavy, dusty person looked into the soiled book and ran his finger down the page.

"That's right!" he announced. "Address all correct. Van on the way around there now."

I hurried back comforted. I do not believe in strong language, but that heavy individual with the soiled book was a dusty liar. There is no other word to express it—if there was, and a stronger one, I would use it. He was a liar by instinct and a prevaricator by trade. The van was not at our door when I returned. Neither had it started in our direction.

We had expected to get down to our new quarters by noon and enjoy a little lunch at a near-by restaurant before putting things in order. At lunch time the van had still not appeared, and there was no near-by restaurant. The Precious Ones began to demand food and the Little Woman laboriously dug down into several receptacles before she finally brought forth part of a loaf of dry bread and a small, stony lump of butter. But to the Precious Ones it meant life and renewed joy.

The moving man came at one o'clock and in a great hurry. He seemed surprised that we were ready for him. There were so many reasons why he had not come sooner that we presently wondered how he had been able to get there at all. He was a merry, self-assured villain, and whistled as he and his rusty assistant hustled our things out on the pavement, leaving all the doors open.

We were not contented with his manner of loading. The pieces we were proud of—our polished Louis-XIVth-Street furniture—he hurried into the darkness of his mighty van, while those pieces which in every household are regarded more as matters of use than ornament he left ranged along the pavement for all the world to gape at. Now and then he paused to recount incidents of his former varied experience and to try on such of my old clothes as came within his reach. I realized now why most of the things he wore did not fit him. His wardrobe was the accumulation of many movings.

This contempt for our furniture was poorly concealed. He suggested, kindly enough, however, that for living around in flats it was too light, and after briefly watching his handling of it I quite agreed with him. It was four o'clock when we were finally off, and the shades of evening had fallen before we reached our new home.

The generous and sympathetic welcome of our new janitress was like balm. One was low-voiced and her own sorrows had filled her with a broad understanding of human trials. She looked weary herself, and suggested *en passant* that the doctor had prescribed a little stimulant as being what she most needed, but that, of course, such things were not for the poor.

I had a bottle of material, distilled over the peat fires of Scotland. I knew where it was and I found it for her. Then the moving man came up with a number of our belongings and we forgot her in the general turmoil and misery that ensued. Bump—bump—up the narrow stairs came our household goods and gods, and were planted at random about the floor, in shapeless heaps and pyramids. All were up, at last, except a few large pieces.

At this point in the proceedings the moving man and his assistant paused in their labors and the former fished out of his misfit clothing a greasy piece of paper which he handed me. I glanced at it under the jet and saw that it was my bill.

"Oh, all right," I said, "I can't stop just now. Wait till you get everything up, and then I can get at my purse and pay you."

He grinned at me.

"It's the boss's rule," he said, "to collect before the last things is taken out of the van."

I understood now why the pieces of value had gone in first. I also understood what the "boss" had meant in saying that we would have to get up early to get ahead of him. While I was digging up the money they made side remarks to each other on the lateness of the hour, the length of the stairs, and the heaviness of the pieces still to come. I gave them each a liberal tip in sheer desperation.

They were gone at last and we stood helplessly among our belongings that lay like flotsam and jetsam tossed up on a forbidding shore. The Precious Ones were whimpering with cold and hunger and want of sleep; the hopelessness of life pressed heavily upon us. Wearily we dragged something together for beds, and then crept out to find food. When we returned there was a dark object in the dim hall against our door. I struck a match to see what it was. It was a woman, and the sorrows of living and the troubles of dying were as naught to her. Above and about her hung the aroma of the peat fires of Scotland. It was our janitress, and she had returned us the empty bottle.

V.

A Boarding House for a Change.

Our new janitor was not altogether unworthy, but she drowned her sorrows too deeply and too often, and her praiseworthy attributes were incidentally submerged in the process. She was naturally kind-hearted, and meant to be industrious, but the demon of the still had laid its blight heavily upon her. We often found her grim and harsh, even to the point of malevolence, and she did not sweep the stairs.

We attempted diplomacy at first, and affected a deep sympathy with her wrongs. Then we tried bribery, and in this moral decline I descended to things that I wish now neither to confess nor remember.

In desperation, at last, we complained to the agent, whereupon she promptly inundated her griefs even more deeply than usual, and sat upon the stairs outside our door to denounce us. She declared that a widow's curse was upon us, and that we would never prosper. It sounded gruesome at the time, but we have wondered since whether a grass widow's is as effective, for we learned presently that her spouse, though absent, was still in the flesh.

It was at the end of the second month that we agreed upon boarding. We said that after all housekeeping on a small scale was less agreeable and more expensive than one might suppose, viewing it at long range.

We looked over the papers again and found the inducements attractive. We figured out that we could get two handsome rooms and board for no more, and perhaps even a trifle less, than we had been expending on the doubtful luxury of apartment life. Then, too, there would be a freedom from the responsibility of marketing, and the preparation of food. We looked forward to being able to come down to the dining-room without knowing beforehand just what we were going to have.

It was well that we enjoyed this pleasure in anticipation. Viewed in the retrospective it is wanting. We did know exactly what we were going to have after the first week. We learned the combination perfectly in that time, and solved the system of deductive boarding-house economy within the month so correctly that given the Sunday bill of fare we could have supplied in minute detail the daily program for the remainder of any week in the year.

Of course there is a satisfaction in working out a problem like that, and we did take a grim pleasure on Sunday afternoons in figuring just what we were to have for each meal on the rest of the days, but after the novelty of this wore off there began to be something really deadly about the exactness of this household machinery and the certainty of our calculations.

The prospect of Tuesday's stew, for instance, was not a thing to be disregarded or lightly disposed of. It assumed a definite place in the week's program as early as two o'clock on Sunday afternoon, and even when Tuesday was lived down and had linked itself to the past, the memory of its cuisine lingered and lay upon us until we even fancied that the very walls of our two plush upholstered rooms were tinged and tainted and permeated with the haunting sorrow of a million Tuesday stews.

It is true that we were no longer subject to janitorial dictation, or to the dumb-waiter complications which are often distressing to those who live at the top of the house and get the last choice of the meat and ice deliveries, but our landlady and the boarders we had always with us.

The former was a very stout person and otherwise afflicted with Christian science and a weak chest. It did not seem altogether consistent that she should have both, though we did not encourage a discussion of the matter. We were willing that she should have as many things as she could stand up under if she only wouldn't try to divide them with us.

I am sure now that some of the other boarders must have been discourteous and even harsh with this unfortunate female, and that by contrast we appeared sympathetic and kind. At least, it seemed that she drifted to us by some natural process, and evenings when I wanted to read, or be read to by the Little Woman, she blew in to review the story of her ailments and to expound the philosophy which holds that all the ills of life are but vanity and imagination. Perhaps her ailments *may* have been all imagination and vanity, but they did not seem so to us. They seemed quite real. Indeed they became so deadly real in time that more than once we locked our doors after the Precious Ones were asleep, turned out the gas, and sat silent and trembling in darkness until the destroying angel should pass by.

I have spoken of the boarders. They too laid their burdens upon us. For what reason I can only conjecture. They brought us their whole stock of complaints—complaints of the landlady, of the table and of each other. Being from the great wide West we may have seemed a bit more broadly human than most of those whose natures had been dwarfed and blighted in the city's narrow soulless round of daily toil. Or it may be all of them had fallen out among themselves before we came. I don't know. I know that a good many of them had, for they told us about it—casually at first, and then in detail.

As an example, we learned from the woman across the hall that another woman, who occupied the top floor back and painted undesirable water-colors, had been once an artist's model, and that she smoked. From the top floor back, in turn, we discovered that the woman across the way, now a writer of more or less impossible plays, had been formerly a ballet girl and still did a turn now and then to aid in the support of a dissolute and absent husband.

These things made it trying for us. We could not tell which was the more deserving of sympathy. Both seemed to have drawn a pretty poor hand in what was a hard enough game at best. And there were others.

Within the month we were conversant with all the existing feuds as well as those of the past, and with the plots that were being hatched to result in a new brood of scandals and counterplots, which were retailed to the Little Woman and subsequently to me. We were a regular clearing-house at last for the wrongs and shortcomings of the whole establishment, and the responsibility of our position weighed us down.

We had never been concerned in intrigue before, and it did not agree with our simple lives. I could feel myself deteriorating, morally and intellectually. I had a desire to beat the Precious Ones (who were certainly well behaved for children shut up in two stuffy rooms) or better still to set the house afire, and run amuck killing and slaying down four flights of stairs—to do something very terrible in fact—something deadly and horrible and final that would put an end forever to this melancholy haunt of Tuesday stews and ghoulish boarders with the torturing tattle of their everlasting tongues. I shocked the Little Woman daily with words and phrases, used heretofore only under very trying conditions, that had insensibly become the decorations of my ordinary speech.

Clearly something had to be done, and that very soon, if we were to save even the remnants of respectability. We recalled with fondness some of the very discomforts of apartment life and said we would go back to it at any cost.

Our furniture was in storage. We would get it out, and we would begin anew, profiting by our experience. We would go at once, and among other things we would go farther up town. So far down was too noisy, besides the air was not good for the Precious Ones.

It was coming on spring, too, and it would be pleasanter farther up. Not so far as we had been before, but far enough to be out of the whirl and clatter and jangle. It was possible, we believed, to strike the happy medium, and this we regarded somewhat in the light of another discovery.

Life now began to assume a new interest. In the few remaining days of our stay in the boarding-house we grew tolerant and even fond of our fellow-boarders, and admitted that an endless succession of Tuesday stews and Wednesday hashes would make us even as they. We went so far as to sympathize heartily with the landlady, who wept and embraced the Little Woman when we went, and gave the Precious Ones some indigestible candy.

We set forth then, happy in the belief that we had mastered, at last, the problem of metropolitan living. We had tried boarding for a change, and as such it had been a success, but we were altogether ready to take up our stored furniture and find lodgment for it, some place, any place, where the bill of fare was not wholly deductive, where our rooms would not be made a confessional and a scandal bureau, and where we could, in some measure, at least, feel that we had a "home, sweet home."

VI.

Pursuing the Ideal.

I suppose it was our eagerness for a home that made us so easy to please.

Looking back now after a period of years on the apartment we selected for our ideal nest I am at a loss to recall our reasons for doing so. Innocent though we were, it does not seem to me that we could have found in the brief time devoted to the search so poor a street, so wretched a place, and so disreputable a janitor (this time a man). I only wish to recall that the place was damp and small, with the kitchen in front; that some people across the air shaft were wont to raise Cain all night long; that the two men below us frequently attempted to murder each other at unseemly hours, and that some extra matting and furniture stored in the basement were stolen, I suspect, by the janitor himself.

Once more we folded our tents, such of them as we had left, and went far up town—very far, this time. We said that if we had to live up town at all we would go far enough to get a whiff of air from fresh fields.

There was spring in the air when we moved, and far above the Harlem River, where birds sang under blue skies and the south breeze swept into our top-floor windows, we set up our household goods and gods once more. They were getting a bit shaky now, and bruised. The mirrors on sideboard and dresser had never been put on twice the same, and the middle leg of the dining-room table wobbled from having been removed so often. But we oiled out the mark and memory of the moving-man, bought new matting, and went into the month of June fresh, clean, and hopeful, with no regret for past errors.

And now at last we found really some degree of comfort. It is true our neighbors were hardly congenial, but they were inoffensive and kindly disposed. The piano on the floor beneath did not furnish pleasing entertainment, but neither was it constant in its efforts to do so. The stairs were long and difficult of ascent, but our distance from the street was gratifying. The business center was far away, but I had learned to improve the time consumed in transit, and our cool eyrie was refreshing after the city heat.

As for the janitor, or janitress, for I do not know in which side of the family the office was existent, he, she, or both were merely lazy, indifferent, and usually invisible. Between them they managed to keep the place fairly clean, and willingly promised anything we asked. It is true they never fulfilled these obligations, but they were always eager to renew them with interest, and on the whole the place was not at all bad.

But the Precious Ones had, by this time, grown fond of change. We were scarcely settled before they began to ask when we were going to move again, and often requested as a favor that we take them out to look at some flats. We overheard them playing "flat-hunting" almost every day, in which game one of them would assume the part of janitor to "show through" while the other would be a prospective tenant who surveyed things critically and made characteristic remarks, such as, "How many flights up?" "How much?" "Too small," "Oh, my, kitchen's too dark," "What awful paper," "You don't call that closet a room, I hope," and the like. It seemed a harmless game, and we did not suspect that in a more serious form its fascinations were insidiously rooting themselves in our own lives. It is true we often found ourselves pausing in front of new apartments and wondering what they were like inside, and urged by the Precious Ones entered, now and then, to see and inquire. In fact the Precious Ones really embarrassed us sometimes when, on warm Sunday afternoons, where people were sitting out on the shady steps, they would pause eagerly in front of the sign "To Let" with: "Oh, papa, look! Seven rooms and bath! Oh, mamma, let's go in and see them! Oh, please, mamma! Please, papa!"

At such times we hurried by, oblivious to their importunities, but when the situation was less trying we only too frequently yielded, and each time with less and less reluctance.

It was in the early fall that we moved again,—into a sunny corner flat on a second floor that we strayed into during one of these rambles, and became ensnared by its clean, new attractions. We said that it would be better for winter, and that we were tired of four long flight of stairs. But, alas, by spring every thing was out of order from the electric bell at the entrance to the clothes-lines on the roof, while janitors came and went like Punch and Judy figures. Most of the time we had none, and some that we had were better dead. So we moved when the birds came back, but it was a mistake, and on the Fourth of July we celebrated by moving again.

We now called ourselves "van-dwellers," the term applied by landlord and agent to those who move systematically and inhabit the moving-man's great trundling house no less than four to six times a year. I am not sure, however, that we ever really earned the title. The true "van-dweller" makes money by moving and getting free rent, while I fear the wear and tear on our chattels more than offset any advantage we ever acquired in this particular direction.

I can think of no reason now for having taken our next flat except that it was different from any of those preceding. Still, it was better than the summer board we selected from sixty answers to our advertisement, and after eighteen minutes' experience with a sweltering room and an aged and apoplectic dog whose quarters we seemed to have usurped, we came back to it like returning exiles.

It was a long time before we moved again—almost four months. Then the Little Woman strayed into another new house, and was captivated by a series of rooms that ran merrily around a little extension in a manner that allowed the sun to shine into every window.

We had become connoisseurs by this time. We could tell almost the exact shape and price of an apartment from its outside appearance. After one glance inside we could carry the plan mentally for months and reproduce it minutely on paper at will. We had learned, too, that it is only by living in many houses in rotation that you can know the varied charms of apartment life. No one flat can provide them all.

The new place had its attractions and we passed a merry Christmas there. Altogether our stay in it was not unpleasant, in spite of the soiled and soulless Teutonic lady below stairs. I think we might have remained longer in this place but for the fact that when spring came once more we were seized with the idea of becoming suburbanites.

We said that a city apartment after all was no place for children, and that a yard of our own, and green fields, must be found. With the numerous quick train services about New York it was altogether possible to get out and in as readily as from almost any point of the upper metropolis, and that, after all, in the country was the only place to live.

We got nearly one hundred answers to our carefully-worded advertisement for a house, or part of a house, within certain limits, and the one selected was seemingly ideal. Green fields behind it, a railroad station within easy walking distance, grasshoppers singing in the weeds across the road. We strolled, hand in hand with the Precious Ones, over sweet meadows, gathering dandelions and listening to the birds. We had a lawn, too, and sunny windows, and we felt free to do as we chose in any part of our domain, even in the basement, for here there was no janitor.

We rejoiced in our newly-acquired freedom, and praised everything from the warm sunlight that lay in a square on the matting of every room to the rain that splashed against the windows and trailed across the waving fields. It is true we had a servant now—Rosa, of whom I shall speak later—but even the responsibility (and it *was* that) of this acquirement did not altogether destroy our happiness. Summer and autumn slipped away. The Precious Ones grew tall and brown, and the old cares and annoyances of apartment life troubled us no more.

But with the rigors and gloom and wretchedness of winter the charms of our suburban home were less apparent. The matter of heat became a serious question, and the memory of steam radiators was a haunting one. More than once the Little Woman was moved to refer to our "cosy little apartment" of the winter before. Also, the railway station seemed farther away through a dark night and a pouring rain, the fields were gray and sodden, and the grasshoppers across the road were all dead.

We did not admit that we were dissatisfied. In fact, we said so often that we would not go back to the city to live that no one could possibly suspect our even considering such a thing.

However, we went in that direction one morning when we set out for a car ride, and as we passed the new apartment houses of Washington Heights we found ourselves regarding them with something of the old-time interest. Of course there was nothing personal in this interest. It was purely professional, so to speak, and we assured each other repeatedly that even the best apartment (we had prospered somewhat in the world's goods by this time and we no longer spoke of "flats")—that even the best "apartment", then, was only an apartment after all, which is true, when you come to think of it.

Still, there certainly were attractive new houses, and among them appeared to be some of a different pattern from any in our "collection." One in particular attracted us, and a blockade of cars ahead just then gave us time to observe it more closely.

There were ornamental iron gates at the front entrance, and there was a spot of shells and pebbles next the pavement—almost a touch of seashore, and altogether different from the cheerless welcome of most apartment houses. Then, of course, the street car passing right by the door would be convenient——

The blockade ahead showed no sign of opening that we could see. By silent but common consent we rose and left the car. Past the little plot of sea beach, through the fancy iron gates, up to the scarcely finished, daintily decorated, latest improved apartment we went, conducted by a dignified, newly-uniformed colored janitor, who quoted prices and inducements.

I looked at the Little Woman—she looked at me. Each saw that the other was thinking of the long, hard walk from the station on dark, wet nights, the dead grasshoppers, and the gray, gloomy fields. We were both silent all the way home, remembering the iron gates, the clean janitor, the spot of shells, and a beautiful palm that stood in the vestibule. We were both silent and we were thinking, but we did not move until nearly a week later.

VII.

Owed to the Moving Man.
WRITTEN TO GET EVEN.

He pledged his solemn word for ten,
And lo, he cometh not till noon—
So ready his excuses then,
We wonder why he came so soon.
He whistles while our goods and gods
He storeth in his mighty van—
No lurking sting of conscience prods
The happy-hearted moving man.

Upon the pavement in a row,
Beneath the cruel noonday glare,
The things we do not wish to show
He places, and he leaves them there.
There hour by hour will they remain
For all the gaping world to scan,
The while we coax and chide in vain
The careless-hearted moving man.

When darkness finds our poor array
Like drift upon a barren shore,
Perchance we gaze on it and say
With vigor, "We will roam no more."
But when the year its course hath run,
And May completes the rhythmic span,
Again, I wot, we'll call upon
The happy-hearted moving man.

VIII.

Household Retainers.

It is of Rosa that I would speak now, Rosa, the young and consuming; and of Wilhelmine, the reformer.

Rosa came first in our affections. It was during our first period of suburban residence that she became a part of our domestic economy, though on second thought economy seems hardly the word. She was tall, and, while you could never have guessed it to look into her winsome, gentle face, I am sure that she was hollow all the way down.

When I first gazed upon her I wondered why one so young (she was barely sixteen), and with such delicacy of feature, should have been given feet so disproportionate in size. I know now that they were mere recesses, and that it was my fate for the time being to fill, or to try to fill, them.

She came in the afternoon, and when, after a portion of the roast had been devoted to the Precious Ones and their forbears, and an allotment of the pudding had been issued and dallied over, Rosa came on and literally demolished on a dead run every hope of to-morrow's stew, or hash, or a "between-meal" for the Precious Ones—licked not only the platter, but the vegetable dishes, the gravy tureen, the bread board, and the pudding pan, clean, so to speak.

At first we merely smiled indulgently and said: "Poor thing, she is half starved, and it is a pleasure to have her enjoy a good meal. She can't keep it up, of course."

Rosa.

But this was simply bad judgment. At daybreak I hastened out for a new invoice of bread stuff and market supplies in order to provide for immediate wants. Rosa had rested well and was equal to the occasion. When I returned in the evening I found that our larder had been replenished and wrecked twice during my absence. The Little Woman had a driven, hunted look in her face, while Rosa was as winsome and gentle-featured, as sweet and placid in her consciousness of well being and doing, as a cathedral saint. In fact, it always seemed to me that she never looked so like a madonna as she did immediately after destroying the better part of a two-dollar roast and such other trifles as chanced to be within reach in the hour of her strong requirements.

And these things she could do seven days in the week and as many times during each twenty-four hours as opportunity yielded to her purpose. We were hopeful for days that it was only a temporary disaster, and that we would eventually get her filled up, shoes and all.

But days became weeks and weeks gathered themselves into months. Each morning Rosa came up winsome and glad to be alive—fresh as the dew on the currant bushes and ravenous as a Mohammedan at the end of Ramadan.

It was no use. We gave it up at last, and merely concerned ourselves with getting sufficient unto the day and moment.

But there was another side to Rosa. She was willing to take counsel, in the matter of her labors, and profit by it. Also she had no particular aversion to work, and she was beloved of the Precious Ones. It is true she had no special regard for the fragility of queensware, but care in these matters is not expected even of old retainers; while Rosa, as I have said, was in the flower of youth.

It was not without regret, therefore, that we found she could not accompany us to the city. Her people did not wish her to become a part of the great metropolis in early youth, and were willing to do the best they could with her appetite at home until another near-by source of supplies could be found. So it was that Rosa passed out of our fortunes when we gave up suburban life and became dwellers in the Monte Cristo apartments.

It was then that Wilhelmine came. The Little Woman's brother Tom was to abide with us for a season, and it seemed necessary to have somebody. I suggested that any employment bureau could doubtless supply us with just what we needed, and the Little Woman went down to see.

I have never known exactly what her experiences were there, though she has done her best to tell me. Her account lacked lucidity and connection, but from what I can gather piecemeal, she did not enjoy herself.

However, the experiment resulted in something—a very old German individual in a short dress, stout of person, and no English worth mentioning. She came on us like a cyclone, and her speech was as a spring torrent in volume. I happened to know one or two German words, and when incautiously I chanced to let her have a look at them she seized my hand and did a skirt dance. Then presently she ran out into the kitchen, took everything from every shelf, and rearranged the articles in a manner adapted to the uses of nothing human.

This was the beginning, and relentlessly she pursued her course, backed up by a lifetime of experience, and the strong German traditions of centuries.

The entire household was reorganized under her regime. The Little Woman and the Precious Ones were firmly directed, and I was daily called to account in a mixture of high-geared German and splintered English that was fairly amazing in its quantity.

Nothing was so trivial as to escape Wilhelmine. Like all great generals, she regarded even the minutest details as important, and I was handled with no less severity for cutting an extra slice of bread than for investing in a new rug for the front room. For, let it be said now, Wilhelmine was economical and abhorred waste. Neither did she break the crockery, and, unlike Rosa, she did not eat. She was no longer young and growing, and the necessity of coaling-up every hour or two seemed to have gone by.

But, alas! we would have preferred beautiful, young, careless, larder-wrecking Rosa to Wilhelmine, the reformer. We would have welcomed her with joy, and surreptitiously in whispers we hatched plots to rid ourselves of the tyrant. Once I even went so far as to rebel and battle with her in the very sanctity of the kitchen itself.

Not that Wilhelmine could not cook. In her own German cabbage-and-onion way she was resourceful, and the house reeked with her combinations until strong men shed tears, and even the janitor hurried by our door with bowed head. I never questioned her ability to cook, but in the matter of coffee she was hopeless. In the best German I could muster I told her so. I told her so several times, so that it could sink in. I said it over forward and backward and sideways, in order to get the verbs right, and when she was through denouncing me I said that I would give her an object lesson in making coffee in a French pot.

I am sure now that this was a mistake—that German blood could stand almost anything in the world better than a French coffee-pot, but at the time I did not recall the affairs and animosities of nations.

I had other things to think of. I was employed in the delicate operation of extracting amber nectar by a tedious dripping process, and simultaneously engaging with a rapid-fire German at short range. I understood very little of what she said, and what I did gather was not complimentary. I fired a volley or two at last myself, and then retreated in good order bearing the coffee-pot.

The coffee was a success, but it was obtained at too great a risk. That night we wrote to Rosa and to her mother. We got no reply, and, after days of anxious waiting, the Little Woman went out to discuss the situation in person. But the family had moved, and there had been a very heavy snow. The Little Woman waded about nearly all day in pursuit of the new address. She learned it at last, but it was too late then to go any farther, so she came home and wrote again, only to get no reply. Then I tried my hand in the matter as follows:—

LINES TO ROSA IN ABSENCE.

Lady Rosa Vere de Smith,
Leave your kin and leave your kith;
Life without you is a mockery;
Come once more and rend our crockery.

Lady Rosa Vere de Smith,
Life for us has lost its pith;
You taught us how to prize you thus,
And now you will not bide with us.

Lady Rosa Vere de Smith,
Have we no voice to reach you with?
Come once more and wreck our larder;
We will welcome you with ardor.

I could have written more of this, perhaps, and I still believe it would have proved effective, but when I read aloud as far as written, the Little Woman announced that she would rather do without Rosa forever than to let a thing like that go through the mails. So it was suppressed, and Rosa was lost to us, I fear, for all time.

But Providence had not entirely forgotten us, though its ways as usual were inscrutable. Wilhelmine, it seems, locked herself nightly in her room, and the locks being noiseless in the Monte Cristo apartments she could not realize when the key turned that she was really safely barred in. Hence it seems she continued to twist at the key which, being of a slender pattern, was one night wrenched apart and Wilhelmine, alas! was only too surely fortified in her stronghold. When she realized this she, of course, became wildly vociferous.

I heard the outburst and hastening back found her declaring that she was lost without a doubt. That the house would certainly catch fire before she was released and that she would be burned like a rat in a trap.

I called to her reassuringly, but it did no good. Then I climbed up on a chair set on top of a table, and observed her over the transom. She had her wardrobe tied in a bundle all ready for the fire which she assured me was certain to come, though how she hoped to get her wardrobe out when she could not get herself out, or of what use it would be to her afterwards was not clear.

It was useless to persuade her to go to bed and let me get a locksmith in the morning. I was convinced that she would carry-on all night like a forgotten *dachshund*, unless she was released. It was too late to find a locksmith and I did not wish to take the janitor into the situation.

I got a screw-driver and handed it over to her telling her to unscrew the lock. But by this time she had reached a state where she did not know one end of the implement from another. She merely looked at it helplessly and continued to leap about and bewail her fate loudly and in mixed tongues.

I saw at last that I must climb over the transom. It was small, and I am a large man. I looked at the size of it and then considered my height and shoulder measure. Then I made the effort.

I could not go through feet first, and to go through a transom head first is neither dignified or exhilarating. When I was something more than half through I pawed about in the air head down in a vain effort to reach a little chiffonier in Wilhelmine's room.

She watched me with interest to see how near I could come to it, and by some mental process it dawned upon her at last that she could help matters by pushing it toward me. Having reached this conclusion the rest was easy, for she was as strong as an ox and swung the furniture toward me like a toy.

Five minutes later I had unscrewed the lock and Wilhelmine was free. So were we, for when I threw the lock into a drawer with a few choice German remarks which I had been practising for just such an emergency, Wilhelmine seized upon her bundles, already packed, and, vowing that she would abide in no place where she could not lie down in the security of strong and hard twisting keys, she disappeared, strewing the stairway with German verbs and expletives in her departure.

We saw her no more, and in two weeks, by constant airing, we had our culinary memories of her reduced to such a degree that the flat on the floor above found a tenant, and carbolic acid was no longer needed in the halls.

IX.

Ann.

And now came Ann, Ann, the Hibernian and the minstrel. During the first week of her abode with us she entertained us at dinner by singing a weird Irish love ballad and so won our hearts that the Little Woman decided to take the Precious Ones for a brief visit to homes and firesides in the Far West, leaving her Brother Tom and myself in Ann's charge.

When she went away she beamed upon Tom and me and said, reassuringly, "Ann will take good care of you all right. We were fortunate to secure a girl like Ann on such short notice. Get your lunches outside sometimes; that will please her." Then she and the Precious Ones kissed us both, the bell rang and they were gone.

My brother-in-law and I were doing what we referred to as "our book" at this time, and were interested to the point of absorption. Ann the Hibernian therefore had the household—at least, the back of the household—pretty much to herself.

I do not know just when the falling off did begin. We were both very much taken up with our work. But when, one morning, I happened to notice that it was a quarter of twelve when we sat down to a breakfast of stale bread and warmed-over coffee, it occurred to me that there was a hitch somewhere in our system.

That evening, when it got too dark to work, I arose and drifted out to the kitchen, perhaps with some idea of being hungry, and a mild curiosity to know when dinner might be expected. There was an air of desolation about the place that seemed strange, and an odor that seemed familiar. Like a hound on the trail I followed the latter straight on through the kitchen, to the servants' room at the back. The door was ajar, and the mystery was solved. Our noble Ann had fallen prey to the cup that yearly sweeps thousands into unhonored graves.

We went out for dinner, and the next morning we got our own eggs and coffee. When our minion regained consciousness we reviled her and cast her out.

We said we would get our own meals. We had camped out together and taken turns at the cooking. We would camp out now in the flat. We were quite elated with the idea, and out of the fulness of our freedom gave Ann a dollar and a little bracer out of some "private stock." Ann declared we were "pairfect gintlemen," and for the first time seemed sorry to go.

Both being eager to get back to our work after breakfast, neither of us referred to the dirty dishes, and I did not remember them again until dinner time. Tom got into a tangle with our heroine about one o'clock, and said he would get the lunch by way of relaxation. I presume he relaxed sufficiently without attending to the plates. At least, I found them untouched when I went out to look after the dinner.

I discovered, also, that the lavish Tom had exhausted the commissary to achieve the lunch. I was obliged, therefore, to go at once to the grocery, and on the way made up a mental list of the things easiest to prepare. I would get canned things, I said, as many of these were ready for the table, and some of them could be eaten out of the can. This would save dishes. I do not recall now just what I had planned as my bill of fare, but I suppose I must have forgotten some of it when I learned that our grocer was closing out his stock of wet goods very cheap, for Tom looked at the stuff when it came and asked if I thought of running a bar. I said I had bought with a view to saving dishes. Then he hunted up the cork-screw and we dined.

In spite of my superior management, however, the dish pile in the kitchen sink grew steadily.

On the morning of the third day the china closet was exhausted, and we took down the Little Woman's Crown Derby and blue India plates from their hangers in the parlor.

On the evening of the fourth day Tom got our work into an inextricable tangle, and took a reflective stroll out into the kitchen. He came back looking hopelessly discouraged. On the fifth morning we followed Ann's example.

The atmosphere suddenly cleared now. We reached conclusions by amazingly short cuts, and our troubles vanished like the dew of morning. The next day would be Sunday. We would go into the country for recreation. To-night we would put a line in the paper and on Monday morning we would have another servant. It seemed hardly worth our while to attempt to camp out permanently.

I will pass over Sunday without further comment. The recollection is weird and extravagant. I remember being surprised at finding certain stretches of pavement perpendicular, and of trying to climb them. Still we must have got a line in the paper on Saturday night, for on Monday the bell began ringing violently before we were up. Tom either did not hear it, or was wilfully unconscious. Finally I got up wretchedly and dragged on some garments. There was no ice, so I pressed my head for a few minutes to a marble-topped center table.

I suppose it was because I did not feel very bright that the voices of my guests were not restful to me. I was almost irritated by one shrill-voiced creature who insisted on going through every room, even to our study. Her tone was dictatorial and severe. Still I might have retained her had she not commented disagreeably on the dishes in the kitchen sink.

One after another they followed her example. Every woman of them began to make excuses and back away when she looked at that unwashed china. Most of them perjured themselves with the statement that they had come to see about a place for another girl.

After the initial lot they scattered along through the forenoon. Tom had got up, meantime, and was leaning on the front window-sill watching hungrily for the ice-man.

In the midst of this anguish the bell rang once more, timidly and with evident hesitation, and a moment later I feebly opened the door to admit—Ann!

She was neatly dressed, as when she had first come to us, and there were other gratifying indications of reform.

"Sure an' I saw your advertisement," she began, humbly, "an' I thought two such gintlemen as yerselves moight not be too hard on a daycent woman who only takes a drop or two now an' then———"

I led her back to the kitchen and pointed to the sink. As we passed through the dining-room she noticed the empty bottles on the table and crossed herself. When she looked at the kitchen sink she exclaimed, "Holy Mary!" But she did not desert us. Her charity was greater than ours.

I went in to tell Tom of the renovation and general reform that was about to begin. He had just succeeded in hailing the ice-man and was feeling better. When I went back into the kitchen there was a wash-boiler of water heating on the range.

Just then the postman whistled and brought a letter from the Little Woman.

"I have decided to stay a week longer than I intended," she wrote. "It is so pleasant here, and Ann, I am sure, is taking good care of you."

We had a confidential understanding with Ann that night. She remained with us a year afterward, and during that time the sacred trust formed by the three of us was not betrayed.

X.

A "Flat" Failure.

In the Monte Cristo apartments it would seem that we had found harbor at last. Days ran into weeks, weeks to months, and these became a year, at length—the first we had passed under any one roof. Then there came a change. The house was not so well built as it had appeared, and with the beginning of decay there came also a change of landlord and janitor. Our spruce and not unworthy colored man was replaced by one Thomas, who was no less spruce, indeed, but as much more severe in his discipline as his good-natured employer was lax in the matter of needed repairs.

Every evening, at length, when we gathered about the dinner table, the Little Woman recited to me the story of her day's wrongs. They were many and various, but they may be summed up in the two words—janitor and landlord. The arrogance of one and the negligence of the other were rapidly making life in the Monte Cristo apartments insupportable. Of course there were minor annoyances—the children across the hall, for instance, and the maid in the kitchen—but these faded into insignificance when contrasted with the leaky plumbing, sagging doors, rattling windows and the like on the part of Mr. Griffin, the landlord, and new arbitrary rulings concerning the supply of steam for the parlor, coal for the kitchen range, the taking away of refuse, and the austere stairway restrictions imposed upon our Precious Ones on the part of Thomas, the janitor.

It is true the landlord was not over-exacting in the matter of rent, and when he came about, which was not often, would promise anything and everything with the greatest good-will in the world, while Thomas kept the front steps and halls in a condition which was really better than we had been used to, or than the rent schedule would ordinarily justify. But the good-will of the landlord usually went no farther than his ready promises, while the industry of Thomas was overshadowed by his gloomy discipline and haughty severity, which presently made him, if not the terror, certainly the awe, of Monte Cristo dwellers. We had not minded this so much, however, until when one day the Precious Ones paused on the stair a moment to rest, as was their wont, and were perhaps even laughing in their childish and musical way, Thomas, who had now been with us some three months or more, appeared suddenly from some concealed lurking-place and ordered them to their own quarters, with a warning against a repetition of the offense that seemed unduly somber. It frightened the Precious Ones so thoroughly that they were almost afraid to pass through the halls alone next day, and came and went quite on a run, looking neither to the right nor to the left.

It was then that we said we would go. Of course, moving was not pleasant; we had enough memories in that line already, though time had robbed them of their bitterness, I suppose, for we grew quite cheerful over the idea of seeking a new abiding-place, and it being Sunday, began looking over the advertisement columns immediately after breakfast. I would make a list, I said, and stop in here and there to investigate on the way to and from business. We would get nearer to business, for one thing, also nearer the car-line. We would have a lighter flat, too, and we would pay less for it. We agreed upon these things almost instantly. Then we began putting down addresses. It was surprising how many good, cheap places there seemed to be now. So many new houses had been built since our last move. We regretted openly to each other that we had not gone before. Then we rested a little to find fault with our quarters. We dug over all the old things, and unearthed a lot of new and hitherto concealed wretchedness that was altogether disheartening. We would move at once, we said. Now! This week!

Perhaps I seemed a trifle less cheerful when I returned next evening. The Little Woman must have noticed it, I suppose, for she asked if I wasn't well. I said that I was tired, which was true. I added that a good many landlords were unscrupulous in the matter of advertising, which I can take an oath is also true. I had left the office early and investigated a number of the apartments on my list, at the expense of some nerve-tissue and considerable car-fare. The advertisements had been more or less misleading. The Little Woman said that in the morning she would go.

The Little Woman herself looked tired the next evening—more tired and several years older than I had ever seen her look. She had walked a good many miles—steep stair miles which are trying. In the end she had arrived only at the conclusion that the best apartments were not advertised. She said it would be better to select the locality we preferred and walk leisurely about the good streets until we spied something attractive. She wished we might do so together.

I took a holiday and we pursued this programme. Like birds seeking a new nesting-place we flitted hither and thither, alighting wheresoever the perch seemed inviting. We alighted in many places, but in most of them we tarried but briefly. It was not that the apartments were inattractive—they were almost irresistible, some of them, but even hasty reflection convinced me that it would be inadvisable to invest ninety-five per cent of my salary each month in rent unless I could be altogether certain that the Little Woman and the Precious Ones could modify their appetites and remain quite well.

Being enthusiastic at first, we examined some of these apartments and the Little Woman acquired credit in my eyes as we proceeded. I did not realize until now the progress she had made since the day of our arrival in Gotham nearly four years previous. Her education was complete—she was a graduate in the great school of flat-life, and was contemplating a post-graduate course. Figures that made me gasp and sustain myself by the silver-mounted plumbing left her quite undisturbed. From her manner you would suppose that it was only the desirability of the apartment itself that was worth consideration. She criticised the arrangement of the rooms and the various appointments with an air of real consequence, while the janitor and I followed her about, humble and unimportant, wondering how we could ever have imagined the place suitable to her requirements.

In one place where the rent was twenty-four hundred it seemed almost impossible to find fault. I began to be frightened for the Little Woman, in the thought that now, after all, she really would be obliged to confess that the little trifle of eighteen hundred dollars a year more than we could possibly pay rendered the place undesirable. But a moment later I realized how little I knew her. When we got to the kitchen she remarked, passively, there was no morning sun in the windows. As the apartment faced east, and there was morning sun in the parlor, this condition seemed more or less normal, as the janitor meekly pointed out. But the Little Woman declared she would never live in another place where the kitchen was dark mornings, and turned away, leaving the janitor scratching his head over the problem of making the sun shine from two directions at once and remaining in that position all day long.

Still it was a narrow escape, and we were consuming time. So we contented ourselves after that with merely inquiring the size and price of the apartment of the hall-boy, and passing on. Even this grew monotonous at length, and we gradually drifted into the outer edges of the chosen district, and from the outer edges into that Section wherein we had made our first beginning nearly four years before, the great wilderness lying north of One Hundred and Sixteenth Street. Then we began work in earnest. We looked at light apartments and dark apartments—apartments on every floor, even to the basement. Though many changes had taken place it carried us back to the day of our first experience, and set us to wondering if we really had learned anything after all.

We saw apartments that we would not have, and apartments which, because of our Precious Ones, would not have us. Apartments that ran straight through the house, apartments that, running down one side of the house and back on the other, solved in a manner the Little Woman's problem of having sunlight in both ends of the house at one time.

It was one of these last that we took. The building, which was comparatively new, was located in the middle of the block, on a little square bit of ground, and had on each floor a cozy octagonal hall with one apartment running entirely around it. The entrance steps and halls were not as unsullied as those of our present habitat, but the janitor was a good-natured soul who won us at first glance, and who seemed on terms of the greatest amity with a small boy who lived on the first landing and accompanied us through. We saw also that the plumbing was in praiseworthy condition, and the doors swung easily on their hinges.

To be sure, the price was a trifle more than we were paying in our present apartment, and the location was somewhat farther from business; but we said that a few blocks more or less were really nothing when one was once on the car, which was almost as near as at the old place, and we figured that the slight difference in rent we could save in the gas-bill, though I had a lingering suspicion that to strike a general average of light in the two places would be to cast but slight reflection on either.

The janitor was the main thing—the good-natured janitor and the landlord. We could even put up with slight drawbacks for the sake of an apartment in good condition and the companionable soul down-stairs. Then, too, we were foot-sore in flesh and spirit, and after the day's experiences welcomed this haven as a genuine discovery. We went home really gratified, though I confess our old nest had never seemed more inviting.

I will touch but lightly upon the next few days. I would rather forget the atmosphere of squalor and destitution that pervaded our household when the carpets had been stripped up and we were stumbling about among half-packed barrels upon bare, resounding floors. I do not seek to retrace in detail the process of packing, which began with some buoyancy and system, to degenerate at last in its endlessness into dropping things mechanically and hopelessly into whatever receptacle came first to hand. I do not wish to renew the moments of vehemence and exasperation when our Precious Ones, who really seemed to enjoy it all, clattered about among the débris, or the vague appreciation of suicide that was born within me when, in the midst of my despair, the Little Woman suggested that after all she was afraid we were making a mistake in leaving our little home where we had been happy so long; also that we moved too often, an unusual statement considering the fact that we had been there for more than a year. I told her that she reminded me of my mother, who daily rated my father for keeping them poor, moving, they having moved twice in thirty-eight years. I added that I had seen my mother publicly denounce my father for having left out a broken stew-pot when they moved the last time, some twenty years before.

I will not review these things fully, nor will I recall, except in the briefest manner, the usual perfidiousness of the moving-man, who, as heretofore, came two hours late, and then arranged upon the pavement all the unbeauteous articles of our household, leaving them bare and wretched in the broad light of day while he thrust into the van the pieces of which we were justly proud.

I will also skim but lightly over the days devoted to getting settled. I sent word to the office that I was ill—a fact which I could have sworn to if necessary, though for a sick man my activity was quite remarkable. The Little Woman was active, too, while the Precious Ones displayed a degree of enterprise and talent for getting directly in my chosen path, which was unusual even for them.

We were installed at last, however, and the jolly janitor had given us a lift now and then which completely won our hearts and more than made up for some minor shortcomings which we discovered here and there as the days passed. We named our new home the "Sunshine" apartment and assured each other that we were very well pleased, and when one morning as I set out for the office I noticed that the lower halls and stairway had suddenly taken on an air of spruce tidiness—had been magically transformed over night, as it were—I was so elated that I returned to point these things out to the Little Woman. She came down to the door with me and agreed that it was quite wonderful, and added the final touch to our satisfaction. She added that it looked almost as if Thomas had been at work there. I went away altogether happy.

Owing to the accumulation of work at the office it was rather later than usual when I returned that evening. As I entered I observed on the face of the Little Woman a peculiar look which did not seem altogether due to the delayed dinner. The Precious Ones also regarded me strangely, and I grew vaguely uneasy without knowing why. It was our elder hope who first addressed me.

"On, pop! you can't guess who's here!"

"No," chimed in the echo, "you never could! Guess, papa; just guess!"

As for the Little Woman, she leaned back in her chair and began laughing hysterically. This was alarming. I knew it could not be her brother who had just sailed for Japan, and I glanced about nervously, having in mind a composite vision of my Aunt Jane, who had once invaded our home with disastrous results, and an old college chum, who only visited me when in financial distress.

"Wh—where are—they?" I half whispered, regarding anxiously the portières.

"Here—up-stairs, down-stairs, everywhere!" gasped the Little Woman, while the Precious Ones continued to insist that I guess and keep on guessing without rest or sustenance till the crack of doom.

Then suddenly I grew quite stern.

"Tell me," I commanded, "what is the matter with you people, and stop this nonsense! Who is it that's here?"

The Little Woman became calm for a brief instant, and emitted a single word. "Thomas!"

I sank weakly into a chair. "Thomas?"

"Yes, Thomas! Thomas!" shrieked the Precious Ones, and then they, too, went off into a fit of ridiculous mirth, while recalling now the sudden transfiguration of the halls I knew they had spoken truly. The Little Woman was wiping her eyes.

"And Mr. Griffin, too," she said, calmly, as if that was quite a matter of course.

"And Mr. Griffin, too!" chorused the Precious Ones.

"Mr. Griffin?"

"Why, yes," said the Little Woman. "He bought this house yesterday, and put Thomas over here in charge. He will occupy the top floor himself."

"Oh!"

"And you never saw anybody so glad of anything as Thomas was to see us here. It was the first time I ever saw him laugh!"

"Oh, he laughed, did he?"

"Yes; and he gave us each some candy!" chanted the Precious Ones. "He said it was like meeting home folks."

"Oh, he did?"

"Mine was chocolate," declared our elder joy.

"Mine was marshmallows!" piped the echo.

"Little Woman," I said, "our dinner is getting cold; suppose we eat it."

XI.

Inheritance and Mania.

And now came one of these episodes which sometimes disturb the sequestered quiet of even the best regulated and most conventional of households. We were notified one day that my Aunt Jane, whom I believe I have once before mentioned having properly arranged her affairs had passed serenely out of life at an age and in a manner that left nothing to be desired.

I was sorry, of course,—as sorry as it was possible to be, considering the fact that she had left me a Sum which though not large was absurdly welcome. I did not sleep very well until it came, fearing there might be some hitch in administrating the will, but there was no hitch (my Aunt Jane, heaven rest her spirit, had been too thoroughly business for that) and the Sum came along in due season.

We would keep this Sum, we decided, as a sinking fund; something to have in the savings bank, to be added to, from time to time, as a provision for the future and our Precious Ones. This seemed a good idea at the time, and it seems so yet, for that matter. I have never been able to discover that there is anything wrong with having money in a good savings bank.

I *put* the Sum in a good savings bank, and we were briefly satisfied with our prudence. It gave us a sort of safe feeling to know that it was there, to be had almost instantly, in case of need.

It was this latter knowledge that destroyed us. When the novelty of feeling safe had worn off we began to need the Sum. Casually at first, coming as a mere suggestion, in fact, from one or the other of us, of what we could buy with it. It is wonderful how many things we were constantly seeing that the Sum would pay for.

Our furniture, for instance, had grown old without becoming antique, and was costly only when you reckon what we had paid for moving it. We had gradually acquired a taste (or it may have been only the need of a taste) for the real thing. Whatever it was it seemed expensive—too expensive to be gratified heretofore, but now that we had the Sum——

The shops along Fourth Avenue were literally bulging with things that we coveted and that the Sum would pay for. I looked at them wistfully in passing, still passing strong in my resolution to let the Sum lie untouched. Then I began to linger and go in, and to imagine that I knew a good piece and a bargain when I saw it. This last may be set down as a fatal symptom. It led me into vile second-hand stores in the hope of finding some hitherto undiscovered treasure. In these I hauled over the wretched jetsam of a thousand cheap apartments and came out dusty and contaminated but not discouraged.

I suggested to the Little Woman one day that it would be in the nature of an investment to buy now, in something old and good, the desk I had needed so long. I assured her that antiques were becoming scarcer each year, and that pieces bought to-day were quite as good as money in the savings bank, besides having the use of them. The Little Woman agreed readily. For a long time she had wanted me to have a desk, and my argument in favor of an antique piece seemed sound.

I did not immediately find a desk that suited me. There were a great many of them, and most of them seemed sufficiently antique, but being still somewhat modern in my ideas I did not altogether agree with their internal arrangements, while such as did appeal would have made too large an incursion into the Sum. What I did find at length was a table—a mahogany veneered table which the dealer said was of a period before the war. I could readily believe it. If he had said that it had been *through* the war I could have believed that, too. It looked it. But I saw in it possibilities, and reflected that it would give me an opportunity to develop a certain mechanical turn which had lain dormant hitherto. The Little Woman had been generous in the matter of the desk. I would buy the table for the Little Woman.

She was pleased, of course, but seemed to me she regarded it a trifle doubtfully when it came in. Still, the price had not been great, and it was astonishing to see how much better it looked when I was through with it, and it was in a dim corner, with its more unfortunate portions next the wall. Indeed, it had about it quite an air of genuine respectability, and made the rest of our things seem poor and trifling. It was the beginning of the end.

Some Colonial chairs came next.

The Little Woman and I discovered their battered skeletons one day as we were hurrying to catch a car. They were piled in front of a place that under ordinary conditions we would have shunned as a pest-house. Still the chairs were really beautiful and it was a genuine "find"! I did not restore these myself—they needed too much. I had them delivered to a cabinet-maker who in turn delivered them to us in a condition that made the rest of our belongings look even shabbier, and at a cost that made another incursion into the Sum.

I renovated and upholstered the next lot of chairs myself, and was proud of the result, though the work was attended by certain unpleasant features, and required time. On the whole, I concluded to let the cabinet-maker undertake the heavy lounge that came next, and was in pieces, as if a cyclone had struck it somewhere back in the forties and it had been lying in a heap, ever since.

It was wonderful what he did with it. It came to us a thing of beauty and an everlasting joy, and his bill made a definite perforation in the Sum.

We did not mind so much now. It was merely altering the form of our investment, we said, and we had determined to become respectable at any cost. The fact that we had been offered more for the restored lounge than it cost us reassured us in our position. Most of our old traps we huddled together one day, and disposed of them to a second-hand man for almost enough to pay for one decent piece—a chiffonier this time—and voted a good riddance to bad rubbish.

Reflecting upon this now, it seems to me we were a bit hasty and unkind. Poor though they were, the old things had served us well and gone with us through the ups and downs of many apartments. In some of them we had rocked the Precious Ones, and on most of them the precious Ones had tried the strength and resistance of their toys. They were racked and battered, it is true and not always to be trusted as to stability, but we knew them and their shortcomings, and they knew us and ours. We knew just how to get them up winding stairs and through narrow doors. They knew about the length of time between each migration, and just about what to expect with each stage of our Progress. They must have long foreseen the end. Let us hope they will one day become "antiques" and fall into fonder and more faithful hands.

But again I am digressing—it is my usual fault. We invested presently in a Chippendale sideboard, and a tall clock which gave me no peace night or day until I heard its mellow tick and strike in our own dim little hall. The aperture in the Sum was now plainly visible, and by the time we had added the desk, which I had felt unable to afford at the start, and a chair to match, it had become an orifice that widened to a gap, with the still further addition of a small but not inexpensive Chippendale cabinet and something to put within it.

The Little Woman called a halt now. She said she thought we had enough invested in this particular direction, that it was not wise to put all one's eggs into one basket. Besides, we had all the things our place would hold comfortably: rather more, in fact, except in the matter of rugs. The floors of the Sunshine apartment were hard finished and shellacked. Such rugs as we had were rare only as to numbers, and we were no longer proud of them. I quite agreed with the Little Woman on the question of furniture, but I said that now we had such good things in that line, I would invest in one really good rug.

I did. I drifted one day into an Armenian place on Broadway into which the looms of the Orient had poured a lavish store. Small black-haired men issued from among the heaped-up wares like mice in a granary. I was surrounded—I was beseeched and entreated—I was made to sit down while piece after piece of antiquity and art were unrolled at my feet. At each unrolling the tallest of the black men would spread his hands and look at me.

"A painting, a painting, a masterpiece. I never have such fine piece since I begin business;" and each of the other small black men would spread their hands and look at me and murmur low, reverent exclamations.

I did not buy the first time. You must know that even when one has become inured to the tariff on antique furniture, and has still the remains of a Sum to draw upon, there is something about the prices of oriental rugs that is discouraging when one has ever given the matter much previous thought.

But the memory of those unrolled masterpieces haunted me. There was something fascinating and Eastern and fine about sitting in state as it were, and having the treasures of the Orient spread before you by those little dark men.

So I went again, and this time I made the first downward step. It was a Cashmere—a thick, mellow antique piece with a purple bloom pervading it, and a narrow faded strip at one end that betokened exposure and age. The Little Woman gasped when she saw it, and the Precious Ones approved it in chorus. It took me more than a week to confess the full price. It had to be done by stages; for of course the Little Woman had not sat as I had sat and had the "paintings of the East" unrolled at her feet and thus grown accustomed to magnificence. To tell her all at once that our one new possession had cost about five times as much as all the rest of our rugs put together would have been an unnecessary rashness on my part. As it was, she came to it by degrees, and by degrees also she realized that our other floor coverings were poor, base, and spurious.

Still I was prudent in my next selections. I bought two smaller pieces, a Kazak strip, and a Beloochistan mat. This was really all we needed, but a few days later a small piece of antique Bokhara overpowered me, and I fell. I said it would be nice on the wall, and the Little Woman confessed that it was, but again insisted that we would better stop now. She little realized my condition. The small dark men in their dim-lit Broadway cave had woven a spell about me that made the seductions of antique furniture as a forgotten tale.

I bought a book on rug collecting, and I could not pass their treasure-house without turning in. They had learned to know me from afar, and the sound of my step was the signal for a horde of them to come tumbling out from among the rugs.

It was the old story of Eastern magic. The spell of the Orient was upon me, and in the language of my friends I went plunging down the *rug*ged path to ruin. I added an Anatolian to my collections—a small one that I could slip into the house without the Little Woman seeing it until it was placed and in position to help me in my defense. It was the same with a Bergama and a Coula, but by this time the Precious Ones would come tearing out into the hall when I came home and then rush back, calling as they ran: "Oh, mamma, he's got one and he's holding it behind him! He's got another rug, mamma!"

So when I got the big Khiva I felt that some new tactics must be adopted. In the first place, it would take two strong men to carry it, and in the next place it would cover the parlor floor completely, and meant the transferring to the walls of several former purchases.

Further than this, its addition would make the hole in the Sum big enough to drive a wagon through—a band-wagon at that with a whole circus procession behind it. Indeed, the remains of the Sum would be merely fragmentary, so to speak, and only the glad Christmas season could make it possible for me to confess and justify to the Little Woman the fulness of the situation.

Luckily, Christmas was not far distant. The dark men agreed to hold the big Khiva until the day before, and then deliver it to the janitor. With the janitor's help I could get it up and into the apartment after the Little Woman had gone to bed. I could spread it down at my leisure and decorate the walls with some of those now on the floor. When on the glad Christmas morning this would burst upon the Little Woman in sudden splendor, I felt that she would not be too severe in her judgment.

It was a good plan, and it worked as well as most plans do. There were some hitches, of course. The Little Woman, for instance, was not yet in bed when the janitor was ready to help me, and I was in mortal terror lest she should hear us getting the big roll into the hallway, or coming out later should stumble over it in the dark. But she did not seem to hear, and she did not venture out into the hall. Neither did she seem to notice anything unusual when by and by I stumbled over it myself and plunged through a large pasteboard box in which there was something else for the Little Woman— something likely to make her still more lenient in the matter of the rug. I made enough noise to arouse the people in the next flat, but the Little Woman can be very discreet on Christmas eve.

She slept well the next morning, too,—a morning I shall long remember. If you have never attempted to lay a ten-by-twelve Khiva rug in a small flat-parlor, under couches and tables and things, and with an extra supply of steam going, you do not understand what one can undergo for the sake of art. It's a fairly interesting job for three people—two to lift the furniture and one to spread the rug, and even then it isn't easy to find a place to stand on. It was about four o clock I think when I began, and the memory of the next three hours is weird, and lacking in Christmas spirit. I know now just how every piece of furniture we possess looks from the under side. I suppose this isn't a bad sort of knowledge to have, but I would rather not acquire it while I am pulling the wrinkles out of a two-hundred-pound rug. But when the Little Woman looked at the result and at me she was even more kind than I had expected. She did not denounce me. She couldn't. Looking me over carefully she realized dimly what the effort had cost, and pitied me. It was a happy Christmas, altogether, and in the afternoon, looking at our possessions, the Little Woman remarked that we needed a house now to display them properly. It was a chance remark but it bore fruit.

XII.

Gilded Affluence.

Yet not immediately. We had still to make the final step of our Progress in apartment life, and to acquire other valuable experience. It happened in this wise.

Of the Sum there still remained a fragment—unimportant and fragile, it would seem—but quite sufficient, as it proved, to make our lives reasonably exciting for several months.

A friend on the Stock Exchange whispered to me one morning that there was to be a big jump in Calfskin Common—something phenomenal, he said, and that a hundred shares would pay a profit directly that would resemble money picked up in the highway.

I had never dealt in stocks, or discovered any currency in the public thoroughfares, but my recent inheritance of the Sum and its benefits had developed a taste in the right direction. Calfskin Common was low then, almost as low as it has been since, and an option on a hundred shares could be secured with a ridiculously small amount—even the fragment of the Sum would be sufficient.

I mentioned the matter that night to the Little Woman. We agreed almost instantly that there was no reason why we should not make something on Calfskin Common, though I could see that the Little Woman did not know what Calfskin Common was. I have hinted before that she was not then conversant with the life and lingo of the Stock Exchange, and on the whole my advantage in this direction was less than it seemed at the time. I think we both imagined that Calfskin Common had something to do with a low grade of hides, and the Little Woman said she supposed there must be a prospective demand from some foreign country that would advance the price of cheap shoes. Of course it would be nice to have our investments profitable, but on the whole perhaps I'd better lay in an extra pair or so of everyday footwear for the Precious Ones.

I acquired some information along with my option on the stock next day, so that both the Little Woman and myself could converse quite technically by bed-time. We knew that we had "put up a ten per cent. margin" and had an "option" at twelve dollars a share on a hundred shares of the common stock in leather corporation—said stock being certain to go to fifty and perhaps a hundred dollars a share within the next sixty days. The fragment of the Sum and a trifle more had been exchanged for the Stock, and we were "in on a deal." Then too we had a "stop-loss" on the Stock so that we were safe, whatever happened.

The Little Woman didn't understand the "stop-loss" at first, and when I explained to her that it worked automatically, as it were, she became even more mystified. I gathered from her remarks that she thought it meant something like an automatic water shut-off such as we had in the bath-room to prevent waste. Of course, that was altogether wrong, and I knew it at the time, but it did not seem worth while to explain in detail. I merely said that it was something we could keep setting higher as the stock advanced, so that in event of a downward turn we would save our original sum, with the accrued profits.

Then we talked about what we would do with the money. We said that now we had such a lot of good things and were going to make money out of the Stock we ought to try one really high-class apartment—something with an elevator, and an air of refinement and gentility. It would cost a good deal, of course, but the surroundings would be so much more congenial, so much better for the Precious Ones, and now that I was really doing fairly well, and that we had the Stock—still we would be prudent and not move hastily.

We allowed the Stock to advance five points before we really began to look for a place. Five points advance meant five hundred dollars' profit on our investment, and my friend on the exchange laughed and congratulated me and said it was only the beginning. So we put up the stop-loss, almost as far as it would go, and began to look about for a place that was quite suitable for people with refined taste, some very good things in the way of rugs and furniture, and a Stock.

We were not proud as yet. We merely felt prosperous and were willing to let fortune smile on us amid the proper surroundings. We said it was easy enough to make money, now that we knew how, and that it was no wonder there were so many rich people in the metropolis. We had fought the hard fight, and were willing now to take it somewhat easier. We selected an apartment with these things in view.

It was some difficulty to find a place that suited both us and the Precious Ones. Not that they were hard to please—they welcomed anything in the nature of change—but at most of the fine places children were rigorously barred, a rule, it seemed to us, that might result in rather trying complications between landlord and tenant in the course of time and nature, though we did not pursue investigations in this line. We found lodgment and welcome at length in the Apollo, a newly constructed apartment of the latest pattern and in what seemed a most desirable neighborhood.

The Apollo was really a very imposing and towering affair, with onyx and gilded halls. The elevator that fairly shot us skyward when we ascended to our eerie nest ten stories above the street, and was a boundless joy to the Precious Ones, who would gladly have made their playhouse in the gaudy little car with the brown boy in blue and brass. Our fine belongings looked grand in the new suite, and our rugs on the inlaid and polished floor were luxurious and elegant. Compared with this, much of our past seemed squalid and a period to be forgotten. Ann, who was still with us, put on a white cap and apron at meal-times, and to answer the bell, though the cap had a habit of getting over one ear, while the apron remained white with difficulty.

The janitor of the Apollo was quite as imposing as the house itself,—a fallen nobleman, in fact, though by no means fallen so far as most of those whose possibilities of decline had been immeasurably less. He was stately and uplifting in his demeanor. So much so that I found myself unconsciously imitating his high-born manner and mode of speech. I had a feeling that he was altogether more at home in the place than we were, but I hoped this would pass. Whatever the cost, we were determined to live up to the Apollo and its titled *Chargé d'Affaires*.

And now came exciting days. The Stock continued to advance, as our friend had prophesied. Some days it went up one point, some days two. Every point meant a hundred dollars' clear profit. One day it advanced five full points. We only counted full points. Fractional advances we threw into the next day's good measure, and set the stop-loss higher, and yet ever higher.

We acquired credit with ourselves. We began to think that perhaps after all we hadn't taken quite so good an apartment as we deserved. What was a matter of a thousand dollars more or less on a year's rent when the Stock was yielding a profit of a hundred or two dollars a day. We repeated that it was easy enough now to understand how New Yorkers got rich, and could afford the luxuries heretofore regarded by us with a wonderment that was akin to awe. I began to have a vague notion of abandoning other pursuits and going into stocks, altogether. We even talked of owning our own home on Fifth Avenue. Still we were quite prudent, as was our custom. I did not go definitely into stocks, and we remained with the fallen nobleman in the Apollo. Neither did we actually negotiate for Fifth Avenue property.

The Little Woman bought many papers during the day. In some of them early stock quotations were printed in red, so it might be truly said that these were red-letter days for the Little Woman. When she heard "*Extra!*" being shouted in the street far below she could not dispossess herself of the idea that it had been issued to announce a sensational advance of the Stock. Even as late as ten o'clock one night she insisted on my going down for one, though I explained that the Stock Exchange had closed some seven hours before. The Precious Ones fairly kept the elevator busy during the afternoon, going for extras, and when the final Wall Street edition was secured they would come shouting in,

"Here it is. Look at the Stock, quick, Mamma, and see how much we've made to-day!"

Truly this was a gilded age; though I confess that it did not seem quite real, and looking back now the memory of it seems less pleasant than that of some of the very hard epochs that had gone before. Still, it occupies a place all its own and is not without value in life's completed scheme.

The Stock did not go to fifty. It limped before it got to forty, and we began to be harassed by paltry fractional advances, with even an occasional fractional decline. We did not approve of this. It was annoying to look in the Wall Street edition and find that we had made only twelve dollars and a half, instead of a hundred or two, as had been the case in the beginning. We even thought of selling Calfskin Common and buying a stock that would not act that way; but my friend of the exchange advised against it. He said this was merely a temporary thing, and that fifty and a hundred would come along in good time. He adjusted the stop-loss for us so that there was no danger of the Stock being sold on a temporary decline, and we sat down to wait and watch the papers while the Stock gathered strength for a new upward rush that was sure to come, and would place us in a position to gratify a good many of the ambitions lately formed.

A feverish and nerve-destroying ten days followed. The Stock had become to us as a personal Presence that we watched as it stumbled and struggled and panted, and dug its common Calfskin toes into things in a frantic effort to scale the market. I know now that the men who had organized the deal were boasting and shouting, and beating the air in their wild encouragement, while those who opposed it were hammering, and throttling and flinging mud, in as wild an effort to check and demoralize and destroy. At the time, however, we caught only the echo of these things, and believed as did our friend on the exchange, that a great capitalist was in control of Calfskin Common and would send it to par.

Only we wished he would send it faster. We did not like to fool along this way, an eighth up and an eighth, or a quarter down, and all uncertainty and tension. Besides, we needed our accruing profits to meet our heavily increased expenses which were by no means easy to dispose of with our normal income, improved though it was with time and tireless effort.

Indeed, most of the eighths and quarters presently seemed to be in the wrong direction. It was no fun to lose even twelve dollars and a half a day and keep it up. The Presence in the household was in delicate health. It needed to be coddled and pampered, and the strain of it told on us. The Little Woman developed an anxious look, and grew nervous and feverish at the clamor of an "extra." Sometimes I heard her talking "plus" and "minus" and "points" in her sleep and knew that she had taken the Stock to bed with her.

The memory of our old quiet life in the Sunshine and Monte Cristo began to grow in sweetness beside this sordid and gilded existence in the Apollo. The massive portals and towering masonry which at first had been as a solid foundation for genuine respectability began to seem gloomy and overpowering, and lacking in the true home spirit we had found elsewhere. The smartly dressed and mannered people who rode up and down with us on the elevator did not seem quite genuine, and their complexions were not always real. It may have been the condition of the Stock that disheartened us and made their lives as well as ours seem artificial. I don't know. I only know that I began to have a dim feeling that we would have been happier if we had been satisfied with our oriental rugs and antique furniture, and the remnant of the Sum, without the acquaintance of the Stock and the fallen nobleman below stairs. But, as I have said, all things have their place and value, I suppose, and our regrets, if they were that, have long since been dissipated, with the things that made them possible.

Quickly, as they had come, they passed, and were not. I was working busily one morning in my south front study when the Little Woman entered hurriedly. It was late April and our windows were open, but being much engaged I had not noticed the cries of "extra!" that floated up from the street below. It was these that had brought the Little Woman, however, and she leaned out to look and listen.

"They are calling out something about stocks and Wall Street," she said, "I am sure of it. Go down and see, quick! Calfskin Common must have gone to a hundred!"

"Oh, pshaw!" I laughed, "it's only the assassination of a king, or something. You're excited and don't hear right."

Still, I did go down, and I fumed at the elevator-boy for being so slow to answer, though I suppose he was prompt enough. The "extra" callers had passed by the time I got to the street, but I chased and caught them. Then I ran all the way back to the Apollo, and plunged into the elevator that was just starting heavenward.

I suppose I looked pretty white when I rushed in where the Little Woman was waiting. But the type that told the dreadful tale was red enough, in all conscience. There it was, in daubed vermilion, for the whole world and the Little Woman to see.

"PANIC ON WALL STREET.

"Break in Leather stocks causes general decline. Calfskin Common falls twenty points in ten minutes. Three failures and more to come!"

Following this was a brief list of the most sensational drops and the names of the failing firms. For a moment we stared at each other, speechless. Then the Little Woman recovered voice.

"Oh," she gasped, "we've caused a panic!"

"No," I panted, "but we're in one!"

"And we'll lose everything! People always do in panics, don't they?"

I nodded gloomily.

"A good many do. That is, unless———"

"But the stop-loss!" she remembered joyfully, "we've got a stop-loss!"

"That's so!" I assented, "the stop-loss! Our stock is already sold—that is if the stop-loss worked."

"But you know you said it worked automatically."

"So it does—automatically, if—if it holds! It must have worked! I'll telephone at once, and see."

There was a telephone in the Apollo and I hurried to it. Five women and three men were waiting ahead of me, and every one tried to telephone about stocks. Some got replies and became hysterical. One elderly woman with a juvenile make-up and a great many rings fainted and was borne away unconscious. A good many got nothing whatever.

I was one of the latter. The line to my brokers was busy. It was busy all that day, during which we bought extras and suffered. By night-fall we would have rejoiced to know that even the original fragment of the Sum had been saved out of the general wreck of things on the Street.

It was. Even a little more, for the stop-loss that had failed to hold against the first sudden and overwhelming pressure, had caught somewhere about twenty, and our brokers next morning advised us of the sale.

It was a quiet breakfast that we had. We were rather mixed as to our feelings, but I know now that a sense of relief was what we felt most. It was all over— the tension of anxious days, and the restless nights. Many had been ruined utterly. We had saved something out of the wreck—enough to pay the difference in our rent. Then, too, we were alive and well, and we had our Precious Ones. Also our furniture, which was both satisfactory and paid for. Through the open windows the sweet spring air was blowing in, bringing a breath and memory of country lanes. Even before breakfast was over I reminded the Little Woman of what she had once said about needing a home of our own, now that we had things to put in it. I said that the memory of our one brief suburban experience was like a dream of sunlit and perfumed fields. That we had run the whole gamut of apartment life and the Apollo had been the post-graduate course. In some ways it was better than the others, and if we chose to pinch and economize in other ways, as many did, we still might manage to pay for its luxury, but after all it was not, and never had been a home to me, while the ground and the Precious Ones were too far apart for health.

And the Little Woman, God bless her, agreed instantly and heartily, and declared that we would go. Onyx and gilded elegance she said were obtained at too great a price for people with simple tastes and moderate incomes. As for stocks, we agreed that they were altogether in keeping with our present surroundings—with the onyx and the gilt—with the fallen nobleman below stairs and those who were fallen and not noble, the artificial aristocrats, who rode up and down with us on the elevator. We had had quite enough of it all. We had taken our apartment for a year, but as the place was already full, with tenants waiting, there would be no trouble to sublet to some one of the many who are ever willing to spend most of their income in rent and live the best way they can. Peace be with them. They are welcome to do so, but for people like ourselves the Apollo was not built, and *Vanitas Vanitatum* is written upon its walls.

XIII.

A Home at Last.

We began reading advertisements at once and took jaunts to "see property." The various investment companies supplied free transportation on these occasions. It was a pleasant variation from the old days of flat hunting. The Precious Ones, who remembered with joy our former brief suburban experiment, appreciated it, and raced shouting through rows of new "instalment houses" with nice lawns, all within the commutation limits. We settled on one, at last, through an agency which the trolley-man referred to as the "Reality Trust."

The cash-payment was small and the instalments, if long continued, were at least not discouraging as to size. We had a nice wide lawn with green grass, a big, dry cellar with a furnace, a high, light garret, and eight beautiful light rooms, all our own. At the back there were clothes-poles and room for a garden. In front there was a long porch with a place for a hammock. There was room in the yard for the Precious Ones to romp, as well as space to spread out our rugs. We closed the bargain at once, and engaged a moving man. Our Flat days were over.

And now fortune seemed all at once to smile. The day of our last move was perfect. The moving man came exactly on time and delivered our possessions at the new home on the moment of our arrival there. The Little Woman superintended matters inside, while I spread out my rugs on the grass in the sun and shook them and swept them and scolded the Precious Ones, who were inclined to sit on the one I was handling, to my heart's content. Within an hour the butcher, the baker, and the merry milk-maker had called and established relations. By night-fall we were fairly settled—our furniture, so crowded in a little city apartment, airily scattered through our eight big, beautiful rooms, and our rugs, all fresh and clean, reaching as far as they would go, suggesting new additions to our collection whenever the spell of the dark-faced Armenians in their dim oriental Broadway recess should assert itself during the years to come.

OUR GARDEN FLOURISHED.

Sweet spring days followed. We fairly reveled in seed catalogues, and our garden flourished. Our neighbors, instead of borrowing our loose property, as we had been led to expect by the comic papers, literally overwhelmed us with garden tools and good advice. We needed both, certainly, and were duly thankful.

As for the Precious Ones, they grew fat and brown, refused to wear hats and shoes when summer came, and it required some argument to convince them that even a fragmentary amount of clothes was necessary. All day now they run, and shout, and fall down and cry, and get up again and laugh, sit in the hammock and swing their disreputable dolls, and eat and quarrel and make up and have a beautiful time. At night they sleep in a big airy room where screens let the breeze in and keep out the few friendly mosquitoes that are a part of all suburban life. We are commuters, and we are glad of it, let the comic papers say what they will. The fellows who write those things are bitten with something worse than mosquitoes, *i. e.*, envy—I know, because I have written some of them myself, in the old days. Perhaps it *is* hard to get to and from the train sometimes—perhaps the snow *may* blow into the garret and the lawn be hard to mow on a hot day. But the joy of the healthy Precious

Ones and of coming out of the smelly, clattering city at the end of a hot summer day to a cool, sweet quiet, more than makes up for all the rest; while as one falls asleep, in a restful room that lets the breeze in from three different directions, the memories of flat-life, flat-hunting, and janitors—of sweltering, disordered nights, of crashing cobble and clanging trolleys, of evil-smelling halls and stairways, of these and of every other phase of the yardless, constricted apartment existence, blend into a sigh of relief that is lost in dreamless, refreshing suburban sleep.

XIV.

Closing Remarks.

To those who of necessity are still living in city apartments, and especially to those who are contemplating flat life I would in all seriousness say a few closing words.

It requires education to get the best out of flat life. Not such education as is acquired at Harvard, or Vassar, or even at the Industrial or Cooking schools, but education in the greater school of Humanity. In fact, flat living may be said to amount almost to a profession. The choice of an apartment is an art in itself, and, as no apartment is without drawbacks, the most vital should be considered as all-important, and an agreeable willingness to put up with the minor shortcomings of equal value. Sunlight, rental, locality, accessibility, janitor-service, size, and convenience are all important, and about in the order named. A dark apartment means doctor's bills, and by dark I mean any apartment into which the broad sun does not shine at least a portion of the day. Sunlight is the great microbe-killer, and as moss grows on the north side of a tree, so do minute poison fungi grow in the dim apartment. As to locality, a clean street, as far as possible from the business center is to be preferred, and away from the crash of the elevated railway. People are killed, morally and physically, by noise. For this reason an apartment several flights up is desirable, though the top floor is said by physicians to be somewhat less healthy than the one just below.

It is hard to instruct the novice in these matters. He must learn by experience. But there is one word that contains so much of the secret of successful apartment life that I must not omit it here. That word is Charity. I do not mean by this the giving of money or old clothes to those who slip in whenever the hall door is left unlocked. I mean that *larger* Charity which comes of a wider understanding of the natures and conditions of men.

You cannot expect, for instance, that a man or a woman, who serves for rent only, and wretched basement rent at that, or for a few dollars monthly additional at most, can be a very intelligent, capable person, of serene temper and with qualities that one would most desire in the ideal janitor. In the ordinary New York flat house janitors are engaged on terms that attract only people who can find no other means of obtaining shelter and support. Those who would fulfill your idea of what a janitor should do have been engaged for the more expensive apartments, or they have gone into other professions. The flat-house janitor's work is laborious, unclean, and never ending. It is not conducive to a neat appearance or a joyous disposition. If your janitor is only fairly prompt in the matter of garbage and ashes, and even approximately liberal as to heat and hot water, be glad to say a kind word to him now and then without expecting that he will be humble or even obliging. If you hear him knocking things about and condemning childhood in a general way, remember that *your* children are *only* children, like all the rest, and that a great many children under one roof can stretch even a strong, wise person's endurance to the snapping point.

Then there are the neighbors. Because the woman across the hall is boiling onions and cabbage to-day, do not forget that your cabbage and onion day will come on Wednesday, and she will probably enjoy it just as little as you are appreciating her efforts now. And because the children overhead run up and down and sound like a herd of buffaloes, don't imagine that your own Precious Ones are any more fairy-footed to the people who live just below. It's all in the day's endurance, and the wider your understanding and the greater your charity, the more patiently you will live and let live. It was an old saying that no two families could live under one roof; but in flat life ten and sometimes twenty families must live under one roof, and while you do not need to know them all, or perhaps any of them, you will find that they do, in some measure, become a part of your lives, and that your own part of the whole is just about what you make it.

Also, there are the servant girls. We cannot hope that a highly efficient, intelligent young girl will perform menial labor some sixteen hours a day for a few dollars a week and board, with the privilege of eating off the tubs and sleeping in a five-by-seven closet off the kitchen, when she can obtain a clerkship in one of the department stores where she has light, clean employment, shorter hours, and sees something of the passing show; or when, by attending night school for a short time, she can learn stenography and command even better salary for still shorter hours. It requires quite as much intelligence to be a capable house servant as to be a good clerk; and as for education, there is no lack of that in these days, whatever the rank of life. Even when a girl prefers household service, if she be bright and capable it is but a question of time when she will find employment with those to whom the question of wages is considered as secondary to that of the quality of service obtained in return.

So you see we must not expect too much of our "girl for general housework," unless we are prepared to pay her for her longer hours and harder work something approximating the sum we pay to the other girl who comes down in a sailor hat and pretty shirt waist at nine or ten to take a few letters and typewrite them, and read a nice new novel between times until say five o'clock, and who gets four weeks' vacation in hot weather, and five if she asks for it prettily, with no discontinuance of salary. All this may be different, some day, but while we are waiting, let us not forget that there are many things in the world that it would be well to remember, and that "*the greatest of these*" and the one that embraces all the rest, "*is Charity!*"

Milton Keynes UK
Ingram Content Group UK Ltd.
UKHW030743071024
449371UK00006B/600